The Yes Factor

New Life and Renewal in Sixteen Churches

Edited by James A. Taylor

Compiled by Clair Woodbury

THE UNITED CHURCH PUBLISHING HOUSE

The Yes Factor:
New Life and Renewal in Sixteen Churches

Canadian Cataloguing in Publication Data

Main entry under title:

The yes factor : new life and renewal in sixteen churches

Includes bibliographical references.

ISBN 1-55134-060-7

1. Church growth - United Church of Canada.
2. Church renewal - United Church of Canada.
I. Taylor, James, 1936-   . II. Woodbury, Clair.

BX9881.T49 1996   287.9'2   C96-931594-5

The United Church Publishing House
3250 Bloor St. West, 4th floor
Etobicoke, Ontario, Canada
M8X 2Y4
(416) 231-5931

Cover illustration: Michael Engel

Printed in Canada

960250 ♻

Contents

Preface

1989 saw the beginning of a five year research project sponsored by the Ventures In Mission Fund of the United Church. St. Stephen's College gave the project a home, and asked me to be the director. Each year we crossed Canada on a quest for insights into how congregations are launched and what makes them thrive.

The results were published in ten research reports, available from St. Stephen's College, and summed up in the publication *Called Into Being*, distributed by The United Church Publishing House.

While we were collecting data we heard countless stories of courage, of faith, of pushing ahead against odds. We found people who had literally moved mountains in order to establish an arm of The United Church of Canada in their community. We found people who were in love with their church, and proud to let anyone know it.

We asked some of those people to put the story of their journey in writing. Sixteen answered the challenge, and this volume is the result.

You will find excitement here, the sadness that comes when a beloved church burns, the anticipation when a congregation grows. You will find people meeting the challenges of the '90s, and a lot of people wondering what the next decade will bring. Most of all, you will meet United Church people from coast to coast who will warm your heart and, if you are anything like me, make you proud to be a member of this great United Church of Canada.

Jim Taylor took on the task of editing the rough copy (and some of our writing was pretty rough) into readable text. He has done that with a mastery that deserves our richest thanks.

Enjoy.

Clair Woodbury
Edmonton, Alberta
August 1996

Introduction

In the 1980s The United Church of Canada undertook a major fundraising campaign — called Ventures In Mission — that eventually brought in more than $40 million. Approximately $15 million was used to restructure the United Church's pension plan. The remaining $25 million was allotted to a revolving fund that by 1996 had assisted over 80 new church development and church redevelopment projects. As the loans are repaid to the fund, money becomes available again for new projects.

Ventures In Mission was a dream that arose from three realities — the need to strengthen and establish ministries that reach out to people with special needs, such as the elderly, homeless, unemployed, imprisoned, and terminally ill; the need to establish new congregations and renovate existing worship facilities; and the need to support ongoing pension obligations in a way that did not divert Mission and Service Funds.

In the late 1970s, many congregations found themselves in communities that were changing. These changes reflect the fact that Canada is becoming increasingly urban and multicultural. Extra funds were needed to help congregations that were prepared to take on the challenge of serving their neighbours in new and creative ways.

In 1979, a New Church Development consultation was held with representatives from every Conference. Thirty-eight new church projects were identified as priorities and another 54 were projected for development in the early 1980s.

Before 1955, a combination of pension plans was in effect. Retired ministers and missionaries drawing benefits from these plans were paying the price in reduced incomes. The church annually had diverted money from the Mission and Service Fund to provide additional benefits and to partially offset inflation. This meant that the money was not available for other important outreach endeavours.

These three factors, congregational redevelopment (including special ministries), new church development, and pensions, were the reason a special appeal was authorized at the 28th General Council held in Halifax in 1980.

In 1982, Ventures In Mission was launched and an objective of $40 million was set for it. Thousands of volunteers became part of a program team and United Church people were invited to respond with their pledged gifts.

Over 70,000 donors from 64 percent of our congregations met the challenge, and by the spring of 1985, the dream had been realized; the target had been exceeded.

It is now time to tell the story once more. On these pages are stories of how congregations were supported in their work with the Ventures In Mission fund. But money is not the key to their successes. Without that elusive "yes factor" known as faith, none of the work of the church would be possible.

Although church rolls seem to show an overall decline in membership and givings, many churches are finding ways to reinvent themselves as a relevant presence in their communities. The word renewal suggests a kind of nostalgia; a hankering for a happier past, rather than a desire to work towards a faithful future. "Transformation" is the new word to describe church renewal. As a church and as a society we cannot recapture the "good old days" of the 1950s, described in some of the stories in this book, when Sunday school enrolment was overflowing church capacity, and the church seemed to be the hub of community activity.

However, a "spiritual hunger" seems to have started to replace the "material hunger" of the 1980s. There are many people currently "outside" the church who want to be moved, who want to be touched, who want to be "inside" a spiritual community. There is a vital role for the church to play in the communities of the 1990s as we prepare to move into the next millennium. The "yes factor" is the key to getting us there.

The Yes Factor

Arson forced the congregation of Trinity United in Vernon, B.C. to settle some long-simmering tensions. In the process, they learned to call in outside expertise to help them work out creative solutions to their problems.

Rising from the ashes

by BUNNY VYVYAN

After the Trinity United youth group had met on August 29th, 1985, one of the members stayed behind to help clean up. The young fellow was apparently concerned that the community was not paying enough attention to the church, an institution he considered crucially important. In his troubled mind, it seemed, the best solution was to do something spectacular to attract some attention from the community. So he set a fire in the sanctuary before he left.

The alarm went off about midnight. By the morning of August 30th, all that was left of the building was the front door, a few shaky walls, and lots of smoking ashes.

Brian Jackson, one of Trinity's two ministers, recalls that night vividly. He was up most of the night trying to salvage as much as possible from the building. At the time, he was living in the old manse adjacent to the church property, and was disturbed by the RCMP knocking at his door to get the keys to open the church doors so the fire department could get in to investigate a reported fire. Brian wondered why they didn't just break down the door, but at that time the fire was barely visible. No one realized that it was burning up into the shavings that had been used for insulation in the ceilings of the old building. Ironically, the front door was still intact after the fire had burned out.

Len Harbour, Trinity's senior minister, was also called out. The two ministers and a number of members of the congregation stood and watched their church burn. By some form of grapevine, many people had been notified that their church was on fire. Everyone was still hoping that it was a small fire and could be easily contained, but as the blaze spread through the ceilings and flames kept breaking out in other places, the watchers began to realize that valuable church records could be lost.

Rob Seaton, a church member and a volunteer fire-fighter, offered to go in through the window of the office wing and throw down to the people below whatever he could see that seemed valuable. The secretary, Donna Peaker, had to be escorted in by the fire chief the next morning while parts of the building were still burning and water was dripping everywhere, to rescue any church records that had escaped the flames.

The fire settled unresolved disputes

One of the most traumatic events that a congregation can experience is having their sanctuary burned to ashes. Arson forced us to ponder seriously the lines from the Lord's Prayer: "Forgive us our trespasses as we forgive those who trespass against us." What we now call "The Fire," with capital letters, forced the congregation of Trinity United Church to decide what kind of people of God they wanted to be in the future and what kind of witness they wanted to make in their community.

Vernon is a city of about 23,000 people nestled in the hills at the north end of the beautiful Okanagan Valley. Including the surrounding residential and agricultural areas, it serves a population of around 45,000. Originally a ranching and fruit-growing area, it has more recently become a choice location for retirees and for those wanting to escape the increasing crime and skyrocketing cost of accommodation in coastal communities near Vancouver.

Over the years a number of churches have grown up in Vernon. At one time (when the population was much smaller) 27th Street was known unofficially as Church Street because it had 12 churches in about 15 blocks! Historically, the United Church had attracted the largest number of members, although in recent years several evangelical churches have forged ahead of the traditional denominations: Roman Catholic, Anglican and United.

Prior to The Fire, however, Trinity United had been growing steadily at a pace comparable to the growth of the city and to the growth rate of other United Churches across Canada. As with many similar-sized churches, that growth was not without its fair share of growing pains.

For about five years before The Fire, Trinity had been wrestling with the separate but interrelated problems of staffing and finances. Unfortunately the problems seemed to develop such intensity that they were beginning to cause serious rifts — amongst members of the congregation, between congregation and clergy, and between clergy staff members themselves.

Defusing the clergy crisis

On the surface, things seemed to be fairly serene, but to those connected with the inner workings of the church it was obvious that there had been frustration building up between the two ministers over division of responsibility. A chronic shortage of money for operating expenses didn't ease the tensions. Some members of the congregation felt that the answer was just to let one of the ministers go. However, with only one United Church to serve more than 800 families, the responsibility of ministering to a congregation that large was felt to be too much for one person.

In an attempt to modernize the church organization and make it more efficient, the Official Board, guided by the clergy, restructured the administrative system. They eliminated the Session and the Elders and created a combined body, the Council, to replace these two groups.

Other changes were made in the worship service at this time. Three Sundays a month incorporated innovative forms of worship; the fourth Sunday continued to be the traditional service. This pleased some members of the congregation who were pushing for change, while at the same time it antagonized others who wanted to retain the familiar structures of the past.

This struggle of change versus tradition seemed to be going on in many churches across the country at that time, and was not necessarily limited to the United Church or to Vernon.

Finally, in an attempt to resolve the staffing deadlock, both ministers offered to resign, paving the way for the congregation to hire a consultant to do a leadership review. Ivan Cumming, then executive secretary of B.C. Conference, was sent by the conference office in Vancouver to tackle this job. Although they did not realize it at the time, the people of Trinity had begun to establish a pattern of seeking outside help for impartial assessment and conflict resolution.

Recognizing that the style of leadership of its ministers was crucial to growth and harmony in the congregation, the Pastoral Relations Committee took a long and careful look at the choices for the new minister. The search was brought to a conclusion when the Rev. Len Harbour was called in October of 1983.

Len Harbour was definitely the right person in the right place at the right time. He provided strong leadership firmly grounded in United Church procedures and beliefs, and his organizational skills were impressive. His confident leadership style gave people in the congregation a model to follow to do what needed to be done, an asset that was to become crucial in the near future.

One of the first tasks Len tackled was to work with the Pastoral Relations Committee to call an associate minister. The committee contacted Mr. Brian Jackson, a diaconal minister, whom Len had worked with in Hamilton Conference. As Len told Brian in a telephone interview, "This congregation needs to be loved back to wholeness and I think you're the person to do it." In February 1984, Brian Jackson became part of the Trinity team. Because Len and Brian had known each other before and knew each other's strengths, they soon slipped into an easy and complementary relationship.

Fixing the finances

Len's next big challenge was tackling Trinity's precarious financial problems. Because he was so familiar with the structure and services of The United Church of Canada, Len knew that the national Department of Stewardship Services had the expertise to help. Stewardship assigned Russel Clark to work with the congregation, to re-examine the stewardship of its time, talents and money. This was another link in the pattern of seeking objective outside help in problem solving.

Russel saw that the level of stewardship in the congregation had not changed in a long time. He organized about 125 volunteers for an Every Family Visitation that produced some interesting results. One of the findings was that the church rolls were quite out-of-date and the number of members and adherents did not truly reflect the number of people who considered themselves to belong to Trinity. Armed with a more realistic number of members, the visitation teams helped many people identify gifts and talents that had not been acknowledged before and even gathered in about 70 new members.

As a result of this direct contact, Trinity began to move towards being a more open and participatory congregation.

By the beginning of 1985, things looked as if they were finally going ahead at Trinity. The financial statement for 1984 showed finances finally "in the black" for the first time in many, many years. Both ministers had committed themselves to a long-term pastorate; they were making plans for the future expansion of the church's programs and facilities. Plans had even been drawn up for a complete renovation of the two ageing church halls.

Everything seemed to be heading onwards and upwards, until that night when the whole thing went up in flames.

Rebuilding from the ground up

As the church was still smouldering the following morning, the Rev. Paul Robinson of All Saints Anglican Church down the street came to mourn the tragedy and immediately offered the use of the Anglican facilities, with no strings attached, for as long as the United Church wanted to use them. This was the affirmation of a warm relationship with the Anglican congregation that is still evident today.

Many other people, both members of the congregation and people of other denominations, came and stood with tears streaming down their faces, to mourn the loss of Trinity's historic building. All the next day and into the following weeks, there was an outpouring of grief, shock, and in some cases anger from so many parts of the entire community that the congregation and ministers of Trinity began to appreciate what a large part their church had played in the life of Vernon. It became obvious that any future rebuilding plans would have to consider the needs of the whole community, and not just those of the members.

The UCW.(United Church Women) had often been considered the "backbone" of the church. As soon as the fire was out, these determined women began a rescue effort that would continue even after the new church was built. President Nancy Siver gained access to the kitchen and organized a human conveyor belt to pass all the kitchen equipment that was movable out the door and into waiting vehicles to be transported to a storage place. There was never any doubt that the cooking utensils, dishes, cutlery and tablecloths would all be needed to raise money for the new church. Former grumbling about catering

duties would be all but forgotten as the UCW geared up to do their
part in helping to rebuild Trinity.

Five weddings had been scheduled for the Saturday following the
fire, so there was much scrambling to arrange alternate sites for the
services. True to form and with much good humour, the UCW members stood outside the burned-out shell that Saturday holding up large
signs directing the startled wedding guests to the appropriate locations.

As one of the choir members, Ted Strother, observed at a later
congregational meeting, "Adversity seems to bring out our strength
and determination." Although a few members drifted away in despair,
most of the rest resolved to put their time and talents to work as never
before.

The burned-out shell remained for several months owing to an
ongoing dispute with the insurance companies about rebuilding on
the original foundations. The old walls could not be bulldozed down
until everything was settled. Dr. John Graham, chairperson of the
trustees, was trying to settle the insurance claims but it was slow going.

In the meantime, one couple from the church family decided that
Trinity should bear witness to the Christmas season in spite of its mis-
fortunes. David and Lorraine Brotsky were two talented members of
the congregation, Dave through his theatre work with young people
and Lorraine with her beautiful banners and wall hangings. They prepared two large banners to fasten to the old bell tower to proclaim to
passers-by that although Trinity was burned out it was not down and
out.

An act of communal forgiveness

One of the problems to be addressed was that of grieving and getting rid of anger. On the first Sunday after the fire, at a service in the
Anglican church, Len Harbour preached a moving sermon that recognized everyone's shock and sense of loss, but that urged the congregation to put the past behind them and get on with rebuilding an even
better church. Perhaps as a result, there was never any expression of
vindictiveness towards the troubled young fellow who had caused the
damage in the first place. In fact, the Messengers group (children in
Grades 1-3) sent him a letter to say that they still loved him. As Brian
Jackson noted, "How fitting that our children should lead us in an act
of forgiveness!"

After salvaging a number of the church's memorial items, the Memorial Committee summed up the situation in their annual report by saying, "We are memorials — living memorials — and, together, **we are the church**, as our ancestors were. We shall carry on."

Starting over

A congregational meeting was soon arranged at a nearby school to commence planning for re-building. Everyone agreed that this planning should not be rushed and should carefully consider what Trinity's role ought to be in a rapidly growing community.

Some plans had previously been drawn up for renovating the old structure. As a result, some of the preliminary thinking had already been done. The former renovating committee, chaired by Laurie Peaker, launched the new Planning and Building committees with renewed energy.

The emergency situation stimulated participation. Attendance at the initial general meeting was over 190. While this was not even 50% of the people listed on the church rolls, those who came to the various meetings had obviously signed on for the entire voyage. Along with the commitment, a new sense of family was developing.

The general meeting was organized into small discussion groups so that everyone had input into the decision-making process. Many options were discussed at those early planning meetings and at subsequent meetings over the next few months:

- joining permanently with the Anglicans,
- sharing facilities with another church, e.g., the Seventh Day Adventists,
- breaking the congregation into two smaller congregations located in opposite ends of the community,
- rebuilding on the former site,
- finding a new and larger site,
- constructing a senior citizens' high-rise with church facilities on the main floor,
- building a meeting-hall type of structure with flexible seating and all-purpose rooms.

Someone even suggested "a church without walls" — no church building at all. While this suggestion wasn't followed up, it did graphically illustrate the number of choices available, and it helped the congregation to realize that it really did want a building that would be a focus and a statement to the community.

The time required for effective long-term planning provided some of the members of the congregation with an opportunity to experiment with other forms of worship. Pat and Bill Hesketh were the nucleus of a committee that planned and conducted an informal, intergenerational, participatory, alternate-style worship service at the Schubert Centre, a seniors' recreation building. The effort required left the committee exhausted by the end of the year, but the experiment initiated many ideas that were later incorporated into the services in the new church.

The congregation was searching for a site for their annual Pot Luck supper, a tradition on Anniversary Sunday in November. The Mormon Church immediately offered their facilities, one of the many examples of ecumenical co-operation that Trinity experienced during this time of dislocation.

All that fall and winter the planning went on, with Dr. Gordon Mack chairing most of the meetings. One of the first decisions made was to abandon the old site and move as a single congregation to a new and larger site. This resolved the roadblocks created by city building regulations regarding parking space, access, and building set-back restrictions. As Brian Jackson recalled, "It soon became evident that moving to a new site was the only acceptable option."

A large piece of property (4.1 acres) on the slopes of a city hill was purchased for $145,000 and made ready for construction. Architects Michael Hill and Peter Maltby, who had worked on the original renovation plans, were called in to work with the Planning Committee. After six months of drawing, re-drawing, and endless meetings, the architects finally presented to the church members their concrete vision of the future Trinity United Church in Vernon.

The price tag for this ambitious undertaking, including both land and building, came to $1.7 million dollars! Undaunted, 216 members of the congregation voted to go ahead, with only two dissenting votes.

In the meantime, two things had happened to improve the financial situation. The manse had been sold, and the insurance claim had been settled (less a $120,000 penalty for not rebuilding on the previous foundation). Rather than fight a costly legal battle to regain the penalty money, particularly after an insurance lawyer predicted it would be futile, the Trustees decided to take the rest of the insurance money and put it into short-term investments. This proved to be a wise move, as the interest rates were very high at that time, so a great deal of the penalty money was recouped anyway. One of the Trustees observed that the lesson for other congregations was never to have an insurance policy that locks the congregation into rebuilding on the original site.

Breaking new ground

The sod-turning ceremony for the new building took place on October 9, 1986, using the same shovel that had been used for the sod-turning of the old church.

By then, the Planning Committee had been succeeded by the Building Committee, chaired by Stuart Galbraith, a retired school principal who had the time and the organizational skills to direct this phase of the operation. Stuart was assisted by many people, particularly Lloyd Beattie who took on the task of construction supervisor. Through his former Air Force experience in engineering and constructing large projects, Lloyd knew a lot about all phases of building, and he spent many hours over at the building site.

Nearly every week, from sod-turning through laying of the cornerstone until the building was completed, Shirley and Warren Grabinsky walked over the site to record the progress on film. Their record was later turned into a slide/tape presentation, shown after the church was completed and again at Vernon's centennial celebrations in 1992. Their foresight in recording Trinity's history was invaluable.

Even as construction was going on, though, changes were still being made. Could this be added? Could that be deleted because of excess cost? The architects were very patient and accommodating.

One of the things thought by some people to be an unnecessary frill was the large narthex inside the front entrance. Even the initial doubters would now have to admit that this part of the building has become the focal point for the whole church. With its hexagonal shape, clerestory windows, and stained glass panels surrounding the centre lights, it has become the meeting and greeting and information centre for the congregation. As Pat Hesketh summarized, "It's a wonderful place for all the caring and sharing that goes on there." It is also the informal gathering place where coffee and tea are served after Sunday church services, and small receptions often take place there after weddings and funerals.

The narthex leads out onto a brick patio enclosed on three sides by the church walls. The fourth side was originally an ugly clay bank choked with weeds until a small but industrious group of members transformed it into an attractive rock garden complete with stone seat for quiet meditation. There is also a memorial section for scattering the ashes of deceased church family members.

On one side of the central hallway are a series of three meeting rooms that can be used as one or closed off with folding partitions. The windows look out over the city and the surrounding hills. This same view is seen from the office and the ministers' studies on the opposite side of the narthex.

The UCW was thrilled to see their long-awaited kitchen taking shape. They knew that their catering efforts, along with their Fall and Spring Teas and bazaars, would be needed to help pay off the mortgage for the new structure. From the time of the fire until the end of 1993, the UCW contributed a total of $150,761 towards the mortgage fund! For six years in a row they handed over a cheque for $23,000, in addition to their other church commitments. They also purchased many items for the kitchen, including the expensive dishwasher required by health regulations for catering to the public.

During the planning and building stages, it was clearly agreed that no one group would "own" any of the rooms of the new building. This was so that any group would feel comfortable using any of the rooms, for whatever purpose they needed. The sole exception was the kitchen. After all the UCW had done, it was agreed that they had earned the right to oversee the use of that room.

No one appreciated the efforts of the UCW more than long-time church member Emil Anhorn. After hearing that the women found it tiring serving tea while walking on the cement floors of the new church hall, he personally ordered and paid for new floor tiles.

Little by little over the following months and years, other individuals and groups added to the usefulness and beauty of the site. Allen and Cleone Gosset spent many backbreaking hours planting and tending the gardens, but in the process they made Trinity into one of the beauty spots of Vernon. In 1992, the City of Vernon's centennial year, and in several successive years, Trinity United Church received awards for adding to the beauty of the city.

Beginning again in a new church

The first service in the new sanctuary took place on September 27, 1987, a little over two years after the fire. Marion Best, B.C. Conference president, was guest speaker at the dedication service for the new building. She was also to play an important part in getting Trinity to recognize the right path to take in the future, although no one could foresee at that time that there would still be problems in trying to be a harmonious, growing and committed church. Everyone felt justifiably proud of recent accomplishments; no one was looking too far into the coming years.

One of the first actions in the new church was to adopt The Whole People of God curriculum. This co-ordinated the lectionary with the Sunday school study themes, gave the children a sense of being part of the church family, and ensured an organized progression of sermons for three year periods.

Everyone agreed that the new church was beautiful, but the comfortable pews made some feel guilty, even though upholstered pews were actually cheaper than wooden ones. Having a heavy debt hanging over their heads made it difficult for some in the congregation to fully enjoy the new sanctuary. The total debt for land and building was exacerbated by the difficulty in selling the old church property. The city would not allow the church property to be rezoned from residential to commercial, yet the only people willing to purchase it wanted it for commercial purposes. The city council finally agreed to one developer's proposal and the old church property was sold.

At that point, all the money that could possibly be recovered was put towards the loan that had been taken out for building purposes. But there was still a very large debt, and interest on the debt kept accumulating.

This led to new tensions in the congregation. Some people felt that high mortgage payments were simply a fact of life in present times. Others argued that no new initiatives, both in outreach and expansion of internal church programs, could come about until the mortgage was paid off. The church owned the lovely old Camp Hurlburt property on Okanagan Lake. Some members feared that it might be sold to reduce the debt. Another group, who advocated the hiring of a youth minister to attract more young people to the church, was dismayed to hear yet another faction suggesting letting one of the present ministers go, to reduce staff rather than increase it as a means of paying off more of the debt.

It appeared to be time to ask for outside help again.

The congregation calls in a consultant

By the spring of 1988, the Christian Development Committee, headed by Brian Jackson, had already felt it needed to consult with the congregation to determine the direction people wanted to take in the life and work of the church.

Following the directive of a congregational meeting in March 1988, an ad hoc committee was struck to find a suitable consultant, and the committee later added a request to look into the Church Council structure to see why it was having difficulty functioning efficiently. Marion Best was contacted. She agreed to use her consulting expertise to try to identify the strengths and weaknesses of the Trinity situation. She felt that it would be better to examine the workings of the entire church rather than to concentrate on any one part, an assumption that proved to be entirely correct.

In the meantime, Len Harbour's health had been deteriorating. He had brought with him from Ontario a chronic lung condition known as Farmer's Lung, and he had to be rushed to a Vancouver hospital for emergency treatment for a bout of viral pneumonia early in 1987. He survived the ordeal, but when a malignancy was later found in his lungs he was forced to retire from the ministry. He had given his all to the reconstruction of his beloved church and had paid dearly with his health. At Len's official farewell reception in June of 1989, sadness was balanced with happiness as Ted Roworth, a member of Trinity, was sponsored for future ordination.

When the Rev. Bob Thompson was called to replace the Rev. Len Harbour as minister of Trinity in the summer of 1989, one of the stipulations in his calling was that he must be willing to work closely with Marion Best in the revisioning process.

The process was named "Vision and Ventures." It continued in its various phases for nearly two years. As Shirley Grabinsky observed, "When the old church was destroyed, many of the old traditions went with it." In the new church it was time to build new traditions using everyone's vision of what their church ought to be. With the congregation's help, Marion set up committees to receive input from all parts of the congregation. One result was a noticeable shift to a more participatory congregation than ever before.

Revisioning a congregation

The Vision and Ventures program unfortunately did not solve all of Trinity's problems. Perhaps no program ever can. Financial shortfalls caused by economic woes similar to those all across Canada continued to plague the smooth running of the church.

One of the businessmen in the congregation made a chance re-
mark. If twenty people each contributed $5,000, he said, the mort-
gage could be paid off and the interest saved (about $16,000 a year)
would help to pay for a youth minister. Laurie Peaker, who had chaired
the Planning Committee after the fire, took up the notion and organized a Mortgage Buster campaign. A direct visitation raised the required money in a very short time, but unfortunately this was offset
by a drop in the general givings.

The congregation hired a youth minister anyway — one of the positive things to come out of the Vision and Ventures process. Jim Hannah
came to work with the young people of the congregation. Jim was
studying for diaconal ministry, but he was willing to put his considerable musical and dramatic talents to work running the youth group,
teaching a drama group, writing and directing musical productions,
and taking part in the ministry of the clowns — a mime presentation
that adds colour and drama to the worship service.

Every alternate year, a Stewardship Fair is presented in the church
hall to demonstrate to church members and to the general public that
a lot is happening at Trinity United in Vernon. Every church group
sets up a booth to show what they have been doing. The Fair is advertised on local radio stations as a means of attracting new members to
the church, but even the old members are impressed by this concrete
representation of Trinity's life and work.

In 1993, the UCW's display took the form of a tree to symbolize
the main body and the ten working units. Besides their catering, the
UCW does an impressive amount of outreach work: selling cards for
UNICEF, sponsoring a foster child through Foster Parents Plan, selling used stamps for leprosy relief, remembering senior citizens with
birthday cards, quilting, knitting toques and scarves for the street
people served by First United Church in Vancouver, doing mending
and sewing for patients in the extended care wing of the hospital, baking dozens of cookies for the local Food Bank, and supporting Transition House (Vernon's shelter for battered women).

Kindred Spirits, a new group for women of all ages, is also flour-
ishing. It focuses on friendship, mutual support, and study of the lives
of women world-wide and through the ages in this Ecumenical Decade of Churches in Solidarity with Women in Church and Society.

The men have a weekly Fellowship Breakfast, and couples can
attend the Second Fifties Couples Club social activities or participate
in Couples Communication classes or sessions to present and discuss

John Bradshaw's tapes on family issues (*The Core of Spirituality*, *Family Secrets*, and *Homecoming*).

For those who are either facing death or have just experienced the death of a loved one, Life Before Death and Grief Recovery seminars are offered on a regular basis.

Young people in the congregation and in the wider community can attend Sunday school, Youth Group, Drama Group, Messengers, Explorers, Children's Choir, or one of the Cub, Scout, or Venturer groups sponsored by Trinity's Scouting Group Committee.

Those with artistic talents can make banners and paraments or arrange flowers to beautify the church, while those who enjoy music can sing in the Chancel Choir or join the Joyful Noise instrumental group.

Trinity's Adult Learning and Nurture Committee organizes frequent Bible study classes during the day or in the evenings to accommodate all age groups. Often these study groups lead the participants to involvement in faith-in-action projects like those sponsored by the Outreach Committee. These include selling bags of Bridgehead coffee and making after-church soup lunches to finance tools and seeds for Third World countries, organizing a weekend seminar on Aboriginal issues, distributing collection jars for the annual World Food Day project, and sponsoring refugee families.

The Refugee Committee of Trinity received world attention in 1992-93 when it attempted to sponsor and/or expedite the entry into Canada of a group of 104 Vietnamese boat people who had been rescued by the Canadian Navy's HMCS Provider and taken to a refugee camp in the Philippines. Concerted letter-writing campaigns and even personal visits by two people from Trinity's congregation finally resulted in the resettlement of 88 of these refugees in our country.

And now into the future

Despite its serious financial concerns, Trinity continued to grow and develop. Growth always involves change, and once again the congregation decided to call in outside help to lead them through this change. With Brian Jackson's retirement in June of 1996, there was again need to determine Trinity's future directions.

Typically, the congregation has learned to involve outside, objective, help. In this case, Presbytery officer John Robertson led the congregation through the decision-making process of what they want to do next.

A detailed questionnaire completed by the congregation gave the Pastoral Relations Committee a sense of the church family's priorities in choosing Brian's replacement. As a result, Debra Savage, a diaconal minister, was called to Trinity as associate minister in the summer of 1996. Although Jim Hannah had dropped out of his diaconal ministry studies, he stayed on as part-time staff associate in youth ministry.

Some pessimists have labelled the United Church as a dying church. Trinity would more likely agree with John Robertson, who said, "I don't think we're a dying church; I prefer to think we're a changing church."

In the Mission Statement, which they articulated as a culmination of the Vision and Ventures process, the congregation summarized their past and set out their goals for the future in the following credo:

We are Trinity United Church in Vernon:
- We are a community of faith, seeking to understand and to follow God's purpose as shown to us by Jesus.
- The focus of our life is worship, which guides us to inclusiveness in the gathered community and to service toward the wider community.
- As part of The United Church of Canada, our vision grows out of its heritage, struggle, and call.
- Our vision also grows out of the gifts of our members, past and present.
- As we strive and affirm those gifts, we become the body of Christ, made up of many parts.

We live out that faith in inward and outward journey:
- Our inward journey is in a gathered community, which sometimes faces controversy and conflict, but we work toward becoming open, inclusive, and caring, respecting the rights and opinions of others.
- Our outward journey turns us toward the wider community, and we aspire to a more open response to the spiritual and physical needs of that community, seeking to be sensitive in our individual and corporate action.

Bunny Vyvyan is a retired teacher and weekly newspaper columnist. She belongs to the Kindred Spirits women's group at Trinity and sits on the 6th Vernon Scouting Group Committee as Trinity's sponsor rep.

When the bedroom suburbs of Ontario's largest city overwhelm a small village church, things have to change. Pickering Village United Church in Ajax learned a lot of lessons about how to help that change happen smoothly.

2

$\mathcal{J}$ust up the street

by MARY SPROUL

It happened late on Friday afternoon. Pickering Village United Church was scheduled to hold its first service in its brand new $1.6 million building that weekend. The water hadn't been turned on yet. There had been nail-biting suspense over whether or not the town would grant approval for the water hook-up. Without that approval, of course, the opening would have to be deferred.

Frantic efforts were made all that week to gain the necessary license. At what seemed like the last possible minute, the water was turned on.

One of the volunteers working in the building that afternoon recalled the excitement of that moment. Pickering's minister and secretary came running down the stairs calling, "Hurry up, Edith, they're going to flush the toilet!"

They all ran into the washroom. One of the workers pulled the handle. Nothing happened. In stunned silence they held their breath. A pause. Another try. And suddenly, miraculously, water swirled into the bowl and down the drain.

A cheer went up. The water was in... and so were we!

Unwelcome choices

The new church was not a choice we had wanted to make. There were people in the congregation for whom the familiar old red brick structure on Kingston Road had been a part of their lives since birth. They had been baptized, confirmed, and married there. Memories ran long and deep.

The original plan had been to renovate the historic structure. The church, built in 1897, stood very close to an extremely busy road, Highway #2, the old main route between Toronto and Montreal. Traffic was heavy and parking was a problem. The parking lot of the church was not large, and parking along the street was hazardous. At the same time, the community was almost exploding as new housing developments flooded out over former farmland to the east and north, part of the great building boom of the 1980s. Pickering Village, which had actually been incorporated into the Town of Ajax in 1974, was growing faster and further than anyone had imagined a decade earlier.

As a result, the church was beginning to feel the pinch. Two services on Sunday helped to alleviate the problem to a degree, but with a sanctuary that held just over 200 worshippers, even this solution was only partly successful. The Sunday school, meeting each week in a small Christian Education building behind the church, was crowded to the point where it was becoming more and more difficult to keep the program effective. The Nursery was held in the basement of the church. With less than adequate soundproofing, the effect on the quieter moments of the service upstairs can be imagined! All organizations within the church were hard pressed to find space for mid-week meetings, and the congregation was severely limited in the number of community groups it could accommodate.

Forced into choices

One Saturday evening in the fall of 1992, a room full of people gathered to celebrate and reminisce about the move. One of the highlights was a guitarist who could neither play nor sing very well, but who entertained the crowd with new words to the old "The Battle Hymn of the Republic." A couple of the verses went like this:

There was a church sat on the road and a busy road it was,
There were cars and trucks and vans and cabs, a steady stream because
The village was expanding, there were people everywhere,
It was the eighties and the place was going wild.

The children in the Sunday school were stacked up several deep,
The aisles were full of chairs on Christmas Eve and Easter week.
The babies in the nursery sang descant to all the prayers,
And the UCW ladies had their own quite desperate cares.

The song did not, of course, tell the whole story. But there was more truth than fiction in these lines.

All of this overcrowding raised serious questions in a church that had always enjoyed a reputation for friendliness and commitment to the community. Pickering had a long tradition as a servant church, one that looked and worked beyond itself. Not only had the church for years sponsored and accommodated groups such as the Boy Scouts and Girl Guides, but individual members of the congregation had served on such organizations as the Red Cross, Community Care, the Board of Directors of the local hospital, the Library Board, the United Way, and the Women's Inter-Church Council of Canada. One of the largest Amnesty International groups in Canada was founded here by a member of Pickering United. And over the years we had consistently surpassed our proposed givings to the Mission and Service Fund.

By 1985, though, it had become apparent that, if the church was to uphold this tradition and continue to grow in faith and service, something would have to be done. So it was that, at the congregational meeting early that year, a New Church Development (NCD) Committee was appointed to research the feasibility of (a) renovating and enlarging the existing facility, or (b) selling the property, purchasing another site, and building a new church.

Planning was delayed when our current minister announced that he had accepted a call to another church. The search for a new minister took priority over anything else at that stage. After a mercifully short gap of seven months, Howard Zurbrigg was covenanted as our new minister. The congregation quickly gained momentum again, and by the spring of 1986 the NCD committee had resumed its duties, proceeding methodically in its research of the two options — renovation, or selling and building. At this point no one was in a hurry.

Renovations ruled out

Then suddenly, the pace picked up. In June of 1986, the committee learned of the potential for Ventures in Mission (VIM) financing, if the congregation could get an application in on time. There was a deadline. We learned later that there is almost always a deadline, for everything! With only a short time to pull together all the necessary documentation, the committee swung into high gear.

The presentation prepared for VIM included statistics of the demographics of this area, our own projections of future growth, and the congregation's "Mission Statement and Strategy." Writing this document proved to be one of the most positive things that the committee did as it planned for the future. At first some thought that the Mission Statement was merely something that had to be done as part of our VIM loan application, but it became instead the core of the whole planning process. It gave us a guide, something to help keep us on track through all the changes to come. As one member remarked, "Let's not go through all this and end up with only a building. Let's be sure we know where we're going with it." The strategies outlined in this application made it very clear that Pickering United intended to remain a church that, while strengthening its own inner life, would still actively reach out to others.

Discussions across the broad spectrum of the congregation had shown that the majority of the members favoured staying in their present location. So, in October, an architect was hired to plan the renovation and enlargement of the existing facilities. This plan, adopted by the congregation in January of 1987, became the basis of successful loan applications to both VIM and Presbytery. Our course of action seemed to be set. The NCD committee was replaced by two new committees, the Church Expansion Building Committee and the Church Expansion Campaign Committee, and the planning continued.

Then, quite unexpectedly, things hit a roadblock. The Campaign Committee announced that the original plan, as attractive as it had seemed at the outset, was not feasible. There were too many problems, financial and otherwise. The money that could be raised and pledged by the members, even with the loans from VIM and Presbytery, was not going to be adequate; and the site itself was problematic. However much we loved the old church, it was in a bad location, too close to a busy highway with too little space available for parking. If we carried through on the renovation, we would end up with a huge debt and a facility that still fell far short of meeting our needs.

The plan to renovate was abandoned.

This was a difficult thing to do. A great deal of creative effort, and considerable money, had gone into the planning process for nearly two years. No one wanted to give up the dream of staying put, of reworking and expanding the familiar old church. The decision to look at other options was not lightly made. The remarkable thing is that, in spite of the letdown, there was still a willingness to start again. Those who had put so much into the planning process showed real character in the way they swallowed their disappointment, picked up the pieces, and started over.

With yet another new committee, the Church Expansion Options Committee, the process began again. Between mid-December of 1987 and early March of 1988, this group held fifteen meetings; they explored several possible options, and eventually determined that a move "up the street" was viable. Three acres of land, not far north on Church Street and still within the boundaries of the village, were made available to the congregation for the princely sum of one dollar by a generous local developer, himself a deeply committed Christian. The old property was sold. Both VIM and Presbytery approved the change in plans. By the spring of 1988 the congregation was committed to the new venture.

In a move both practical and symbolic, the church at this point made a decision to change its name. Pickering United became Pickering Village United, and the official ground-breaking ceremony took place on a sunny September afternoon.

Living with the chaos of construction

It had taken three and a half years to get this far. There were moments when we could hardly believe ourselves what we were doing — a congregation of 350 families setting out to build a church at least four times the size of the original at a cost of $1.6 million.

Construction began in October of 1988. From then until the first church service was held in the new facility, on September 10, 1989, the pace never slackened. We had just eleven months to get the job done.

Anyone who has ever been involved in a building project of this magnitude will understand the frustrations and the excitement that go with the territory. There were moments of exasperation and moments of exhilaration; times when we thought we'd never do it (not on time and not within budget, at any rate), and times when we could see the light at the end of the tunnel so clearly that we knew without a doubt that we were going to make it. Some things were done well, others we should have done differently. But one fact we all agree on — it was never dull.

From the beginning of this venture, one of the things that kept our spirits up was that the congregation was kept well informed of developments *before* they had to make major decisions. Initially, everyone had been given a questionnaire, asking what their priorities were. The New Church Development Committee asked every organization in the church, "Tell us your dreams. What do you see in the future for your group?" The young people even had a swimming pool in there for a while! All this information was fed into the hopper right from the start, and as a result people were excited about what was going to happen.

At every step, the NCD committee took pains to communicate their ideas directly to the congregation. They would present a position paper, share information, and invite questions, with no decisions to be made that day. A week later at a follow-up meeting, there would be further opportunity for questions. Only then would people be asked to make a decision. This gave people time to talk with others about concerns and to think things through before having to cast a vote.

Keeping people informed and involving them in the decision-making process was a key part of the strategy from beginning to end of the project. This, of course, meant frequent — very frequent — meetings! In fact, we met so often that one member of the congregation was heard to say, after we'd closed one session with the Mizpah Benediction, "The Lord won't have much watching 'between me and thee' to do. We're never absent one from the other anyway!" He was only half joking.

Even so, things didn't always run smoothly. Not everyone was comfortable with every decision. There was, for instance, heated debate on whether or not a gymnasium should be included in the plan. For some, the increased cost seemed difficult to justify. Strong feelings were expressed on both sides. But when the vote was taken the gym was left in. Five years later, with the congregation greatly increased and community involvement incredibly expanded, we can see that this was the right decision to make.

Although this method of decision making was not always easy, even downright touchy at times, everyone had an opportunity to speak to the issues. A democratic procedure was followed wherever possible. In doing things this way we drew upon one of the strengths of this congregation, one that had been demonstrated many times over the years, the ability to disagree without holding a grudge. Once decisions were made, disagreements were set aside and business moved forward.

Volunteers do their part

As construction began, congregational involvement took on an added dimension. The construction site became a hive of activity as volunteers contributed thousands of hours of work, helping with everything from hammering the rafters in place to hauling refuse to the local dump. The contractor could not believe the amount of work done by the volunteers. Their contribution exceeded by 1,500 hours the best volunteer effort the contractor could recall on any other church building project. A rough estimate calculated a saving of at least $50,000 just in construction costs.

At least another $50,000 was saved when an army of volunteers did the painting. This was no mean feat! All of the woodwork had to be sanded, stained and finished. Metal doors and frames, covered with cement and dirt, had to be scraped, primed, and given three coats. The cement block walls in the basement had to be "scrubbed" and smoothed before being painted. In all, over 500 gallons of paint were used on the inside of the building. It was a monumental task.

Keeping costs down was very important, but there was an additional payoff. As hard as the work was, people still had fun doing it. Even some newer families pitched in, and everyone enjoyed the fellowship of such a "goodly companie." Those who were not able to do hard physical work contributed by baking goodies for the workers. There was something for everyone.

Fellowship was one positive by-product. Another was that volunteers gained a sense of real ownership in the project. Later, those who had laboured with paint brushes and rollers could be heard to say proudly, "That's my wall!"

Every congregation includes members with special talents, abilities, and "connections." We recognized early on how valuable these individuals were. Talents showed up that we had never known existed! We learned that our church was (and still is) endowed with people who represent a wide range of backgrounds and professional training; some are still active in the work force, others have kept themselves active after retirement. In the early stages of development, the fact that we had men and women who were competent planners was crucial — economists and accountants used to doing long range projections and presenting information in an understandable, graphic way. As time went on, we discovered those with skills in other fields. Two of the men on the building committee wired the sound system. Another assisted in making the 17 chandeliers for the sanctuary and narthex. Some unsung heroes showed true grit when they put on their hard hats and rubber boots and dug the mud out of clogged drainage tiles. In late fall and winter, this was no picnic! One of the church families with a useful "connection" assisted us by providing all the paint we needed at cost.

Of course, not every question that arose as the project unfolded could be handled by members of the congregation. There were times when we needed professional advice that was not available within our church family. In choosing the quality and colour of the rug, for instance, the Building Committee looked to outside experts for advice. Because there was so much broadloom involved, over 1400 square yards of it, the committee realized the importance of the decision. Should we upgrade from the contractor's suggested rug? What colour, to complement the oak pews? And what colour paint should go on the walls? These were decisions that everyone would have to live with for years; no one on the committee felt qualified to make them. Outside consultants were brought in and although this meant an added cost, in the long run everyone agreed that it was money well spent. We couldn't always go it alone.

So, valuable lessons were learned, and practiced, as the building materialized. First, we learned that communications can't be too good! Meetings may not be everyone's favourite pastime but the people who are going to end up living with, working in, and paying for the end product must be consulted as much as possible. Second, by having volunteers involved in all phases of the project tremendous advantages are realized: money is saved, fellowship fostered, and ownership taken by all. And finally, we learned that sometimes seeking outside, professional help may be necessary.

Some always deserve special commendation

It's not easy to single out individual church members for commendation because so many contributed so much. But three people in particular did make a tremendous difference as construction progressed. Doug Sproul was responsible for liaison with the contractor, representing the church's interests and seeing that everything was done well, that a high standard of workmanship was maintained. This turned out to be almost a full-time job. Fortunately, he was retired and able to spend long hours both at the site and away from it: monitoring progress, making snap decisions when necessary, insisting on things being redone if there were flaws, checking invoices, phoning suppliers. He could be found up on scaffolds, down in trenches, anywhere that work was being done that day. Any church contemplating a building project should have such a liaison person appointed before construction ever starts. His, or her, role is crucial.

Vern Balsdon saved hundreds of dollars in the long run through his efforts as the treasurer of the Board of Trustees. Working closely with the liaison person, he kept tight control on every aspect of the finances. Every invoice was checked; discounts for prompt payment were taken advantage of; money was never taken out on loan until absolutely needed; and a spreadsheet was updated continually, showing what had been budgeted for all items and how much had been spent at any given time. It was not just a lucky coincidence that the project was completed within budget. Tight financial control was the key.

Marilyn Brewer was the woman who organized the painting. With dozens of volunteers involved, and the added complication of various paints, stains, and procedures to contend with, it took a keen mind and a diplomatic manner to keep everything going smoothly. The job took months. People got tired, and it wasn't easy to keep up the enthusiasm.

One other key player needs to be named here as well, and that is the minister. Howard Zurbrigg was very much involved in the planning and development process from the beginning. Throughout the confusion of selling and moving, even as he participated fully in the development process, he saw to it that congregational life carried on as normally as possible. His job was made even more difficult because the manse he lived in was sold as part of the old church property. That meant, for him, a personal as well as a corporate move. Having a minister who stayed with us through the whole project and who had such exceptional administrative skills — before coming to us, he had been an executive with the Canadian Bible Society — was a great advantage.

The legacy of hasty deadlines

If we were to do it again, are there things that we would do differently? Of course. For one thing, we would spend more time studying the plans of the building before the first shovel ever went into the ground. Because we accepted the architect's plan hastily, without enough critical analysis, we had to make some costly changes after the project was finished.

Almost all areas of the building, including the gym, were initially heated by electricity. This proved so expensive that three years later the congregation voted to convert all but a few rooms to natural gas. The conversion was costly.

The choir loft required changes almost immediately. Choir members found that they could not see the organist, no matter how they positioned themselves. Jumping up on the seats and peeking around each others' heads couldn't be accepted as a long-term solution!

And within a month of moving into the building we discovered that there was not nearly enough storage space.

The heating and the choir loft could be solved with money and extra effort. The lack of storage room, we have had to live with. These three details might have been corrected if we had spent more time studying the architect's drawings before we began to build. Although we managed many things well, we were not quite perfect!

Since 1989 growth in the Village and in the congregation has hardly slowed. In fact, early projections for church growth were exceeded even before the new building was opened. In 1985 there were 275 families under pastoral care; by 1988 that number had increased to 367, and by 1993, to 501. Baptisms increased at an almost alarming rate — 33 in 1985; 66 in 1993! Such rapid expansion led to a second full-time minister being hired within two years of the move. The building, since the day it opened, has been used constantly by church and outside groups, so well used in fact that a separate Bookings Decisions Committee had to be set up in order to keep straight all the comings and goings.

In just five years, Pickering Village went from being a small village church to a much larger, thoroughly urban, church. The challenge has been to retain our friendliness in the midst of all this change. We work hard at this, knowing it to be a characteristic too important to lose.

Arrival in the promised land

The closing date for the sale of the old church was April 30, four months before our new building was to be ready. The main problem became where to store everything. For months items were packed away in people's garages, barns, and basements. Some furniture and boxes could be piled in areas of the new church that were almost finished, but most things were literally all over the place. We sometimes wondered if, like Humpty Dumpty, they could ever get put back together again.

Four months later, when we could actually assemble the parts once more, a procession of cars and pickup trucks began moving up Church Street and into our new parking lot. The procession resembled, we thought, the desert trek of the early Israelites. There was no Red Sea to cross, but carrying everything from Sunday school banners to filing cabinets into our new premises at 300 Church Street North, we couldn't help but feel as though we had finally finished our wandering and come safely through the wilderness to a long-promised land.

It wasn't easy doing without a church home of our own for over four months. During this time our good friends at St. Andrew's Presbyterian Church, not far from the site of our new building, allowed us to use their sanctuary on Sundays for worship services, and other rooms for mid-week meetings as well when necessary. This was a tremendous help. We felt less "dispossessed" when we could meet in familiar surroundings.

In spite of the confusion that reigned at 300 Church Street North, the dust inside and the mud outside, the minister and secretary chose to set up the office there in May, only half completed though it was. There was electricity, of course, but no water in the building. The first flush came much later! The disadvantage of having no "facilities" can be imagined, but there were advantages too. The volunteers saw that their church was not an empty shell. Business was being carried on here; already it was operating as a church.

Because the old church was so special to the members, the final service held there was very emotional. Many tears were shed as we filed out of the church for the very last time on April 30, singing "Lead on, O King Eternal." The last to leave were the minister and the Clerk of Session, carrying the pulpit Bible.

The building had been sold. But we had the foresight to request, under the terms of the sale, the right to remove a few items from the building. These we eventually incorporated into the new facility. Five beautiful stained glass windows were transferred, with great difficulty but fortunately no accidents, and many of the old pews were taken to be installed later in the new chapel. Now, when we sit in our new sanctuary, we see two of the stained glass windows in the chancel area flanking the wooden cross, also brought from the old church. The other windows too were incorporated into the worship area, a beautiful link with the past. On our first Sunday in the new church, the sight of the windows and the cross in the chancel, just as they had always been, lifted everyone's spirits. It was almost like coming home.

Mary Sproul is a retired high school teacher. She has three married children and six grandchildren. She has been an active member of PVUC since 1978 and has served as chair of the Unified Board and the Executive Committee, an elder, a choir member, and chair of the Mission and Service Committee.

McClure United in Saskatoon took its name and its example from the pioneering medical missionary, Dr. Bob McClure. It spent much of its history as "a church without a steeple, serving God by serving people."

3

A base for innovation

by DALE MORRISON

When you approach Saskatoon from the south or east, you can't help noticing a 14-storey, dusty coral apartment tower. It dominates the landscape, looking a little out of place in the centre of a cluster of modern residential neighbourhoods.

If you know nothing about this tower, you might wonder what economic or political considerations determined such an unlikely site. But for those aware of its genesis, the tower is a symbol of the unconventional wisdom, energy, and commitment of the people of McClure United Church.

Dennis and Beth Johnson are charter members of McClure. Back in 1966, they had no intention of moving their membership away from Grosvenor Park United Church, a dynamic faith community that worshipped in a gleaming new sanctuary in the University area. Dennis and Beth both enjoyed their church involvement. They were not aware of plans to establish a new congregation in their burgeoning subdivision until the minister of Grosvenor Park, the Rev. Dr. J. Scott Leith, called them to his office one day to tell them about the new congregation.

"We value your membership here," Leith told the Johnsons. "But that new congregation will need you. We send you out with our blessing."

The Johnsons soon discovered that the same message had been given to some of their friends. "We all felt a bit like missionaries," recalls Beth. "In one way we were reluctant to leave our church home. In another way, we began to feel the excitement of being part of something new."

The formation of a new congregation was a Presbytery initiative. Yet it was evident from the beginning that this would be a congregation with a mind of its own. A sense of mission and a creative, independent spirit were already at work.

Breaking the mould

In its wisdom, Presbytery undertook two actions. One was to purchase land in anticipation of an eventual church building. The other was to appoint an interim minister for the first year. Dennis Johnson says, "These were good decisions, business-like and helpful, even if they were, perhaps, a bit too paternalistic." But neither decision was openly questioned or resented. On the contrary, there was a great deal of enthusiasm for getting off to a running start. In hindsight, however, there was also a desire to break the mould a bit, to try out some new ideas, to do things their own way.

That innovative spirit was evident in the search for a name. A number of conventional suggestions were made. One popular suggestion was "Arlington Avenue United Church" — it had a nice ring to it — because the land Presbytery had acquired was on Arlington Avenue. But Margaret Anderson, who was married to the Superintendent for Home Missions for Northern Saskatchewan, the Rev. Stewart Anderson, suggested instead that the congregation be named "McClure" in honour of the veteran missionary surgeon, Dr. Robert McClure. That idea, she said, had come to her in a dream. In a vote by secret ballot, the name "McClure" received overwhelming approval.

The choice of a name carried with it a powerful subliminal message. It implied service and outreach. It indicated that action was more important than appearance and said it was okay to be unconventional.

In time, Dr. Bob and Amy McClure became personal friends of many in the congregation. Their courage and their faith were immensely influential. During their own lives, Bob and Amy McClure made many decisions that sensible people might have thought foolish, but from their perspective those decisions were simply the natural result of their principles and their faith. That spirit rubbed off on the congregation.

Lay members took leadership

McClure United Church became a close-knit worshipping community of about 200 active households. Towards the end of its formation year, the congregation issued a call to the Rev. Don Johns, then minister of the nearby Viscount pastoral charge. For six years, Don inspired the people at McClure with fine preaching and enabling leadership.

But the key was always lay leadership. Although no one now can recall for sure, it is believed that every Board meeting and every congregational meeting in the entire history of McClure United has been chaired by a lay person. In this way, lay ownership of decisions and accountability for the ongoing work of the congregation became highly valued principles.

To their credit, ministerial staff have always been willing to give lay people room to grow and to learn. Undoubtedly, members of the ministerial team have sometimes had to bite their tongues and be patient while rookie chairpersons struggled to handle their new responsibilities. But they did it, and the congregation grew in confidence in its own abilities as a result.

The congregation adopted, early, the concept of having co-chairs for its Unified Board. This shared leadership has made the chairperson's role somewhat less lonely and somewhat less daunting than it might otherwise have been. It has also allowed for mutual support when new ground needed breaking, or difficult decisions made.

The concept of gender equality has been taken for granted for most of McClure's history. The first co-chair teams were men — that was the standard of the time. But in the last 18 years, only once have the co-chairs both been of the same gender — and in that instance, they were both women. No role in the congregation is seen as being specifically a man's job or a woman's job. The annual fall supper has been most often chaired by a man; the stewardship appeal is often chaired by a woman. Gender-equal planning and programming has developed a multi-talented team of people for any task at hand.

The problems and possibilities of an auditorium

The first service of worship for the new congregation was held in Walter Murray Collegiate on October 20, 1966. A borrowed communion table and pulpit stood on the stage. A number of male ordained members of Presbytery ascended the steps to conduct the service. The people sat in straight rows on hard metal chairs. The chairs elicited a few caustic comments about Pierre Berton's recently published book, The Comfortable *Pew*.

It may have been the last time people sat in straight rows. Over the succeeding years, McClure experimented with all the possible ways one can set up chairs in a square auditorium. Quarter circles, half circles, full circles, clusters — they tried them all. Someone remarked, in those early years, "I wish we could keep things the same for two weeks in a row!"

The urge to experiment was relentless. The lack of pews made experimentation not only possible but sometimes unavoidable. Miscommunication with the caretaker occasionally made improvisation necessary if there was to be a service at all that Sunday morning. Sometimes the chairs were locked in another part of the building; they had to be located first, then transported to the auditorium. Everyone got involved — children and adults rushing along the hallways carrying maximum loads.

Gradually, the most common arrangement for the chairs evolved into a semicircle, with the communion table placed symbolically at the centre. There were never more than eight rows of chairs. One could look around the room and see faces, rather than the backs of people's heads.

Though ministers changed over the years, the emphasis on lay leadership continued. Its strength was perhaps most tested when the Rev. R. J. (Bob) McLellan, who had been called to McClure in 1973, was diagnosed with cancer. People were greatly moved by his courage and faith. Throughout the long months of his illness, McClure members comforted and supported the McLellan family and each other.

Bob McLellan died in the spring of 1978. The grieving congregation struggled to maintain its life and vision. A young teacher, Gary Loy, was chairing the worship committee at the time. The sensitivity with which Gary and others provided worship leadership enabled the congregation not just to survive, but to emerge from its crisis stronger and more focused than ever before.

It was a year and a half before the Rev. Frederick Seller was called to minister with the congregation. During the intervening period, the laity had developed a new level of self-confidence.

In search of identity

Any congregation worshipping in a school auditorium or any other public building has a visibility problem. That was true for McClure. You could not point to something, and say, "There's McClure United Church."

Even in Presbytery, there was a tendency to overlook the existence of McClure. An official committee report, written several years after the congregation was founded, read: "There are only two United Churches east of Cumberland Avenue." In fact there were three: McClure, and two other congregations that had visible church buildings.

Rather than feeling immobilized or marginalized by this lack of recognition, the McClure congregation began a deliberately different kind of lifestyle and ministry. Because they were not burdened by mortgages and property maintenance, they made outreach a key feature of their church life from the beginning. Members of McClure became heavily involved in a city-wide ecumenical organization called "FISH," which provided the kind of help that a caring neighbour would give in response to minor domestic emergencies. Individuals and couples signed up to be on call, one day a month. Problems ranged from simple ones like needing a ride to a doctor's office, to more complex ones:

- An elderly woman called late one afternoon saying that she had to vacate her apartment that day, and the moving company had just informed her they were overbooked and wouldn't be able to do the job.
- A man whose wife had just left him needed somewhere to stay overnight with his two children; he had to work a night shift, and his boss had told him that if he didn't show up, he'd be fired.
- A teenage boy, struggling with his homosexuality, needed someone to talk with.

One advantage of FISH was that it promoted working as couples — something that, oddly enough, was not true of much church work at that time. FISH became a channel for McClure couples to serve together, and at the same time helped them enhance their own relationship.

Through their involvement in community organizations, McClure members established a reputation for being energetic and committed. When Mary Ballentyne received Saskatoon's Citizen of the Year Award in 1981, she commented that she felt she was representing a large number of McClure people who had worked alongside her in FISH and other service programs.

Through those early years, there was still an underlying expectation that someday McClure would construct a church building. Typically, the innovative approach of the congregation led to lengthy and positive discussions with the neighbouring Holy Spirit Roman Catholic Church. The Holy Spirit parish also worshipped in a school, and also had plans to build. Perhaps the two churches could share a sanctuary and other facilities? The prospects for a joint venture looked promising for a while, until eventually the Roman Catholics decided their needs would be better served by building on their own.

The decision was disappointing for members of McClure who had worked long and hard to make this ecumenical venture succeed.

Despite banners, portable worship centre furniture, and carefully arranged chairs, the auditorium of Walter Murray Collegiate never did meet the worship needs of some in the congregation. When negotiations with the Roman Catholics ended, some people left McClure in search of a more traditional church. Those who stayed on did so because they believed that the way in which a congregation expresses its faith and the way it uses its resources matter more than the place where it meets for worship. This group gradually realized that despite steel stacking chairs, overcrowded storage rooms, banging hot water pipes, temperamental caretakers, inadequate church school facilities, and rigid hours when the building was available — or not available — the auditorium somehow felt like "home."

In 1974, some ten years after the congregation was founded, it was decided to sell the parcel of land on Arlington Avenue. The decision did not come easily. It took long, soul-searching deliberations, and Presbytery's permission.

It seemed as if McClure United would remain in the school auditorium forever.

Not everyone was happy about this turn of events. A decade later, 90-year-old Elizabeth Robinson wagged a finger at a church member visiting at her home and exclaimed in her best Irish accent: "I have no been back there for service since the vote. I'd 'a been willin' to bake many a pie to pay off the mortgage if they'd just built a real church!"

Giving away a windfall profit

Though Presbytery had originally purchased the land, McClure had paid the property taxes through the years. Therefore, when the land was sold after ten years of inflation, the two bodies had a windfall profit to share.

It would have been tempting to put the congregation's share of that profit into the local budget. Like most churches, McClure's financial picture was chronically tight. Fortunately, that didn't happen. In 1975, it was decided to have a series of celebrations marking the 50th Anniversary of The United Church of Canada. Events were planned that would help people to appreciate the history of the United Church, to think about its present programs, and to look forward to the future.

Furthermore, the congregation decided to initiate a number of innovative fund-raising projects. For every new dollar raised, a matching dollar would come from the "land fund" — the profit from the sale of the Arlington Avenue property — and the whole amount given away. One third went to a development project in Lesotho, one third to an Anti-Poverty Credit Union, and one third to help retire the debt at the local Friendship Inn, an inner city hospitality centre.

This anniversary project was fun. It was worthwhile. And it felt good!

At the time when the plight of the Vietnamese "boat people" was receiving world-wide attention, McClure applied to sponsor a family. On a cold, windy day in October 1979, a family group of three young men and one young woman got a warm and tearful welcome at the Saskatoon airport. The congregation fully supported the family during their first year in Canada. Some of them, and their families in turn, have found an ongoing place in McClure church.

Since then, the congregation has also sponsored a family from South Africa and individuals and groups from El Salvador. McClure members Ken and Shirley Britton, Ernie Woolf, and Neil Pechey have earned a reputation for being knowledgeable consultants on refugee issues.

As time went on, McClure United Church began to discover its real mission — to serve others. Particularly after the land sale, McClure became increasingly referred to as an outreach church. Someone, in a light-hearted mood, even composed a slogan:

McClure, a church without a steeple,
serving God by serving people.

The slogan may have been a bit corny, but it captured the essence of the congregation's developing sense of identity.

In terms of volunteer labour, most of McClure's outreach work was done locally. In terms of financial support, most of its contribution went nationally or internationally through the Mission and Service Fund of The United Church of Canada. It's hard to quantify outreach. For example, an analysis in 1984 showed that, compared to most other United Churches in Saskatoon, McClure's total givings per household, for all purposes, were roughly on par. They weren't particularly noteworthy — not much more, not much less than others. But the givings to the Mission and Service Fund were the highest in the city — 3.5 times the Saskatchewan average.

For some time, McClure has had an unofficial goal — that 50% of its annual operating budget should go to outreach. That goal has never been reached. The highest it reached was 35%; and it has dropped well below that from time to time. But the 50% goal still stands as an ideal. It serves as a constant reminder that there is still much to be done.

The city keeps on growing

By 1983, McClure United Church had experienced almost two decades of life on the edge of the city. A lively program of worship, Christian education, service and fellowship flourished, still in rented or borrowed space. The church office, a tiny one-bedroom rented apartment, was a busy place. A half-time secretary, Marion Pope, typed the Sunday bulletin on a cranky old manual typewriter, kept an ancient Gestetner working, and maintained the records and minutes of the congregation's Board and committees. Sometimes Marion also baby-sat the children of young parents who came for morning Bible study. Sometimes she tried to work while a committee sat in the same room discussing current church business.

Most committee meetings, though, were held in members' homes. Much of the social life of the congregation focused on these meetings. Often visiting continued long after agenda items had been dealt with.

This style of church life served the congregation well for a number of years.

But the city of Saskatoon had not stopped growing. Bulldozers were preparing new stretches of prairie east of the community for new housing developments. More and more people from those areas were looking to McClure as their home church.

To cope with the growing numbers, a committee was appointed to find larger office and meeting space. About the same time, in the winter of 1983, Saskatoon Presbytery's New Church Development Committee agreed to conduct a series of three workshops for the McClure congregation, to consider ways in which the United Church might reach out to people in the newly established neighbourhoods. The workshops raised several possibilities:

- A new congregation could be formed east of Circle Drive, with McClure continuing its worship life in Walter Murray Collegiate.
- A satellite congregation could be formed, and a two-point pastoral charge established.
- The McClure congregation could move to a new location, east of Circle Drive.

None of these possibilities drew much enthusiasm. Nevertheless, there was an awareness that some changes were inevitable. Many McClure members were becoming middle-aged empty-nesters.

Ironically, given its all too obvious shortcomings, there was a strong loyalty to the Walter Murray setting. A change in setting might adversely affect the McClure philosophy of outreach. These concerns mitigated against any idea of changing location. There wasn't much interest in undertaking a church building project.

Discussions were intense and two decisions were made:

- McClure would notify Presbytery that, in consultation with the New Church Development Committee, the congregation would assume responsibility for the new areas east of Circle Drive.
- McClure would seek larger office and meeting space for mid-week activities.

A new idea grabs imaginations

A number of McClurites gathered in the home of Beth and Dennis Johnson to discuss the future of the congregation. Margaret McKechney, since ordained as a United Church minister, startled the group by suggesting that its next outreach project might be to sponsor a senior citizens' housing project. "It would be an outreach project to be proud of," she insisted. "It would meet a real need in the community."

By the next Sunday morning, Dennis Johnson, who had taken her idea very seriously, was passing out a one-page proposal for a seniors' housing complex that would include both worship and activity space for the McClure congregation.

Dale Morrison, who had just accepted a call to McClure, was in the congregation that Sunday morning. Dale glanced at the page and gasped. He had been involved in the initial stages of the development of a housing project in Winnipeg. Clearly, life at McClure would not be dull!

The winds of change were blowing. Or, as some would say, "the Holy Spirit was moving among us." But sometimes the Holy Spirit seemed very far away. The harsh reality of just how much time and energy the project would take began to dawn on the congregation.

First, there was a door-to-door survey of the entire area, done in co-operation with St. Stephen's Anglican Church. Potential members of both the Anglican and United Church were identified, and the results of the survey were made available to other denominations as well.

Then there came endless meetings with architects, with representatives of the provincial and civic governments, and with Canada Mortgage and Housing Corporation. A private consultant, Marion Jackson (BScN, MSN), determined the feasibility of constructing an enriched senior citizens' housing complex.

The project got a boost when the United Church's capital development program, Ventures in Mission, provided funds for a half-time outreach worker to make connections with people of United Church background in the growing south-east corner of Saskatoon.

Throughout the process, there was consensus within the congregation that any housing project would have to offer more than just a place for seniors to live. It would have to include such services as nursing care, recreational facilities, meals, and social care — all designed to enable residents to live independently longer.

Before long, 50 volunteers had signed up to participate in designing an enriched housing project that would fill a real need in the community and that was in tune with McClure's outreach philosophy. For June Schnell and Muriel Baxter, this was their first involvement in a housing project. Whatever they and the other planners didn't know at the beginning, they made it their business to find out. The architect, Allan Duddridge, sat through hundreds of hours of committee meetings, as the project began to take shape. He listened patiently to the volunteers, and drew dozens of ever-changing sketches.

Meanwhile, the congregation took out an option on a parcel of land at the corner of McKercher Drive and Taylor Street. The funds to buy the option were raised over one weekend in the fall of 1983.

Excitement began to grow for the project. But the road from plan to fulfilment was anything but straight, and anything but easy. Several times, carefully worked out proposals were rejected or put on hold by the Saskatchewan Housing Corporation. Everyone struggled over what to do about including church facilities. Some people thought it would be possible for the church to rent auditorium space from the housing project, just as it had from Walter Murray Collegiate. But it soon became evident that to have enough space, the congregation would have to find the money for its own facilities.

George Baxter, a professor in the Department of Accounting at the University of Saskatchewan, took major responsibility for finances. He gave uncountable hours to the McClure building project. His sense of fairness and integrity caused him to wrestle with every major decision, and his faith and commitment kept him both realistic and adventurous. Would the congregation be able to meet the financial costs of the church portion of the facility? Would the investment of the church, the government, and the residents in the apartment complex, be secure? Questions like those kept George awake at night. The same questions troubled the whole congregation.

A long slow process

The project took six years. Some members of Presbytery began to get impatient. One woman sat in a front row, knitting furiously, during a 1986 meeting when Dennis Johnson was reporting on the status of the project. She was overheard to grumble: "Maybe we should let some people who know what they're doing deal with New Church Development in south-east Saskatoon!" Some critics in Presbytery and in the wider community were openly sceptical. "It's too big an undertaking for a small congregation," they said. "Without significant start-up capital, no government agency will loan you money!"

Dennis just shrugged off the criticisms. "McClure is a great little church," he said calmly.

In the spring and summer of 1988, the pieces finally began to fall into place. The Saskatchewan Housing Corporation gave its approval. Ventures in Mission approved the necessary loans — $600,000 for the church portion of the project. About 135 contributing McClure households pledged over $450,000 in a locally directed fund-raising campaign. The United Church Watkins Fund for seniors loaned start-up moneys, and the balance of the loans necessary to get under way were approved by the Co-op Trust of Saskatoon.

The final plan was to provide 108 apartments for seniors. Of these, 37 units would be subsidized by the Saskatchewan Housing Corporation for rents geared to household income, and 71 would be sold on a life-lease basis.

Heavy equipment moved onto the property in the spring of 1988. Before long, the 14-storey apartment building that had been designed and redesigned many times had begun to grow. Seniors who had already laid claim to their life-lease units drove by every day to monitor progress.

Soon, the steel girders for the church portion of the project appeared nearby. The two buildings would be connected by an indoor link.

No sooner had construction begun than people began to fret about the church being too small. However, when the work was done, it was apparent that this was a facility of which everyone could be proud. Yes, the church was too small to hold the entire growing congregation at one sitting. But knowing that would be the case, advance planning had been done to hold two worship services and two church school programs each Sunday. The church was designed as a multi-purpose building. Space used Sunday morning for worship would be available the rest of the week for everything from carpet bowling to dinner theatre.

On the weekend of May 13-14, 1989, Dr. Bob and Amy McClure, with great pride and joy, presided over the official opening of McClure Place and the dedication of McClure United Church. Bob relished the audacity and commitment of the community that so proudly bore his name.

It was a chilly May Sunday. During the prayers of the people, the overburdened coat rack where the architect and contractor had hung their coats collapsed. But nothing could dampen the enthusiasm and sense of gratitude that pervaded the congregation. Credit belongs to many wonderfully committed and talented people. But perhaps no one experienced a greater sense of satisfaction that particular day than Dennis Johnson, who with remarkable patience and dauntless courage had given oversight to the whole project from start to finish.

New Millennium, New Mission

Now that McClure United has its own worship home *and* seniors' residence, it might be tempting to start resting on its laurels. However a fund-raising campaign, called "A New Millennium, A New Mission," has been launched to eliminate the remaining mortgage on the church by 1999. McClure's innovative spirit and outward view are still an integral part of the congregation's identity.

Settling into a comfortable pew seems out of the question. In this energetic and growing congregation of 850 households people are more interested in what lies beyond paying off the mortgage and in challenging each other, "What can we do next? How can we do it better?"

Dale Morrison is in his fourteenth year of ministry with McClure. He was born in Moose Jaw, Saskatchewan. He is a graduate of St. Andrew's College, past president of Saskatchewan Conference and received a Doctor of Divinity degree from St. Andrew's in 1993.

In its downtown location, Toronto Chinese United was always subsidized by national funds. When it built not one but two suburban congregations, it discovered energies, abilities, and dollars it had never been able to tap before.

4

Releasing untapped energy

by CLAIR WOODBURY

Based on an interview with the Rev. David Lew, former minister, Toronto Chinese United Church.

David Lew is impressive. Thin and tall, he is full of energy as he walks back and forth across his study talking about what it means to be the minister of a Chinese congregation. This is not an ordinary congregation. Toronto Chinese not only built a new church halfway across Toronto from their former downtown location, but also launched a second congregation in Mississauga at the same time.

The Chinese people first came to Canada as railroad builders. When the transcontinental railroad was completed, they became entrepreneurs, first setting up laundries and restaurants. Migration eastward from the west coast eventually reached Toronto. In 1918 the Methodist Church established a mission house in Toronto's Chinatown. It provided facilities for Bible study, classes in English, and recreation — ping pong — to discourage gambling. Later the Board of Home Missions provided a church building.

In those early days the church recruited ministers from China where the United Church was affiliated with the United Church of Christ in China. Ministers came on three year contracts from Canton or Hong Kong. The Board of Home Missions paid their salaries. This process staffed the Canadian Chinese churches, but did little to integrate them into the life of the wider United Church of Canada.

Eventually the Board of Home Missions was dissolved and United Church policy changed so that ethnic congregations related directly to their local Presbytery. At that time the national church transferred the title of the Toronto Chinese Church to the Toronto United Church Council, the property management for the five Toronto-area presbyteries.

Sharing the seed money for new development

In 1985 the Government of Ontario wanted to purchase the land on which Toronto Chinese United stood, in order to build a court house. They had already bought the rest of the block. There were grandiose plans for a whole justice complex — detention centre, justice offices, and court house. The government offer was $2 million. A lot of negotiating went on. Land was expensive at that time in Toronto. If the Toronto Council turned the offer down, the government people said, they would expropriate and pay only $1.5 million — eventually, when all the legal processes ground to an end. The $2 million offer was accepted.

Now the Chinese congregation had to decide where they would go. They asked for the $2 million to build a new church. The counter offer by the Toronto United Church Council was half a million for a piece of land. The Chinese congregation continued to press. In the end they agreed on a 50/50 split of the sale price.

An invitation came from four United Churches in Scarborough, the city at the eastern end of Metropolitan Toronto where there was a growing Chinese population. Ebenezer, St. John's, St. Francis and Knox said the Chinese congregation could use any of the four churches as an interim location. They choose Ebenezer, an old rural church built when that area of Toronto was open farm country.

Preparing the ground, preparing the people

The Toronto Chinese congregation continued to meet in their old location as long as they could, while starting a second satellite congregation in the new area. The two point charge was a challenge to the minister, David Lew. Money was still very tight, and Lew did not even have a secretary, but all in all it worked well.

Lew was preparing the ground in another way while the new church was being built. He established a lay theology class that was more like a junior theological seminary. Lew had taught in a seminary in Hong Kong, so he was no stranger to the classroom. Some 25 lay leaders met every

Saturday afternoon to study Christian beliefs, the Bible, church history, and preaching. When the new church opened, there was going to be trained leadership in it.

Land for the new Toronto Chinese United Church in Scarborough cost $425,000. The final cost for land and building was $2,0210,000. The congregation received an interest free loan for $1 million, to be paid back only if the building was sold. There was another loan at two percent less than prime. In two years enough money was raised to pay that back, and the third year all the remaining debts were cleared off.

But it was not long before the new building began to feel too small. The next phase was a multi-purpose Christian Education wing. It had an assembly hall on the main floor and classrooms on the lower floor. The project cost was $800,000. They had $300,000 raised before the wing was half finished.

In the downtown location, the congregation had spent years on mission support. In Scarborough in a new building, the congregation has not only grown and paid off the initial loan, but has gone on to the next phase of building. The forced sale of their downtown church, while sad in one sense, has been one factor in the revitalization of the congregation.

The new red brick building with the white cross on the front is seldom quiet. A daycare uses the building Monday through Friday. All day Saturday there are classes in Chinese heritage. And on Sunday there are activities from morning right through until the evening.

Why have ethnic congregations at all?

At one time, people questioned the need for ethnic congregations. Immigrants to Canada, went the argument, be they Italian, Hungarian or Chinese, should all learn English, live a Canadian lifestyle, and join the Canadian church — The United Church of Canada.

In 1975 the United Church's General Council passed a resolution that recognized the multi-cultural mosaic nature of Canadian society. There was indeed a valid place for ethnic specific congregations — though the "integration" issue is still raised in various presbyteries from time to time.

The problem with this approach begins with the presbytery itself. Few presbytery officers truly understand the psychology of the Japanese or Chinese or Korean people in their midst. Canadians who have not learned a second language are rarely skilled at working around language differences. As a result, an easy going attitude was often adopted:

"Feel free to do pretty much as you want and take care of your ministry, because we don't know much about ethnic congregations. If you are happy, we are happy." That works until there is trouble. Then presbytery often had no idea how to respond.

David Lew can be very passionate about his church. "It is important to understand the way ethnic congregations develop," he says. "Development is area wide, not local. We are the only ethnic church in Scarborough Presbytery, for example. Scarborough Presbytery will not be able to start a Korean or Japanese church without help from outside."

Statistics tell the story. The United Church of Canada is not very good at starting ethnic congregations. The first Chinese congregation in Toronto was the Toronto Chinese United Church. Seventy-five years later there were almost 100 other Chinese congregations, but still only one Chinese United Church.

At one time there were 13 Chinese United Churches across Canada. Now there are only eight, and one of those is struggling to survive in St. John's, Newfoundland. David Lew has served on the national Ethnic Ministries Committee. His analysis is, "Five Chinese congregations have closed essentially because the local presbytery did not know what to do."

By the end of this century, half of Canada's population will be of non-European descent. The third language used by the most Canadians, after English and French, according to Statistics Canada, is Chinese. People from Hong Kong are pouring in. The church has new faces in the congregation every Sunday. Yet at the present time less than three percent of the congregations in The United Church of Canada are "ethnic." That is the challenge.

Launching a second congregation

The Toronto Chinese congregation had just moved into its new building when the United Church provided $1,500 to study the viability of starting another Chinese ministry in the Golden Horseshoe area. It was an opportunity to start something new, and the Toronto Chinese congregation picked up the challenge.

There were "meetings, meetings, meetings," as David Lew described the process. Finally the recommendation came — Mississauga had the potential to sustain a new congregation. The high cost of housing in the central Toronto area made Mississauga attractive for many new immigrants.

The Toronto congregation chose a number of their leaders who already lived in the Mississauga area and asked them to volunteer as the core group. Altogether about 25 people were selected to start the church. Some could preach, some translate, some play the organ. It was a strong leadership team.

The next question was a location. It may have been just a coincidence, but the idea of starting a new congregation was first raised by Gordon Hume and others in the Division of Mission in Canada. When Gordon resigned from the national office, he became the minister charged with starting a new congregation in Mississauga — Westminster United Church. It seemed like an ideal opportunity to launch the new Chinese congregation in the same location.

Westminster was using a trailer for meetings, and then moved to a nearby high school while their church building was being erected. So the Chinese congregation was also able to start its worship in the trailer. After a year, when the trailer was towed away to make room for the high-rise apartment residence that was part of the total Westminster project, the Chinese congregation also moved into the high school for a year, and finally into the new building with the Westminster congregation.

The spin-off benefits of new energies

One lesson from the experience of Chinese United is the amount of energy unleashed when a congregation moves into a new building. Perhaps it was because the facility is new. Perhaps it was because the new church is located in a community where the founding group was already residing. Or it might have been the way leadership training was taken seriously. The energy involved in launching a new congregation in Mississauga had its own impact on the sponsoring congregation in Scarborough. Whatever the individual factors, they add up to a high energy level and an exciting future for the Toronto Chinese United Church.

Clair Woodbury is the Executive Director of the Canadian Centre for Congregational Life and the co-author of Ministry as an Art *(United Church Publishing House, 1996).*

David Lew retired from active ministry but is serving as the interim minister for the Mississauga Chinese United Church.

Participation in a congregational vitalization program led Scarboro United Church in Calgary to build, not an edifice but a community. It led them from more or less comfortable and isolated complacency into active involvement in their urban social setting.

Reaching out to a wider world

by Susan Murphy and Enid Holtby

April 27, 1991, was an overcast but mild day in Calgary, Alberta. The air had a moist rich smell of green shoots shooting, buds swelling, and bulbs erupting through carpets of wet leaves. It was the sort of day that sees keen gardeners heading for the nursery to get a sneak preview of the new varietals and to dream of blossoming glories in the months to come.

Inside Scarboro United Church, a new kind of life was beginning. The 70 people assembled were involved in another kind of dreaming. We were participating in Visioning Day — the culmination of over a year's work in a congregational vitalization program.

It wasn't a particularly inspiring setting — a gymnasium scarred by years of floor hockey action and a stage framed by the same dusty velvet curtains that had heralded Christmas pageants from time immemorial. Nonetheless, the excitement in the air was palpable as the scent of spring outside.

At the request of the Visioning Day leaders, we affiliated ourselves with one of the four "windows of opportunity" for new or expanded ministry:

- Worship/Celebration
- Learning/Nurture
- Support/Service
- Advocacy

For months we had explored the defining moments of our history, the realities of our present situation, and the implications of our theology. Now we had the opportunity to try to answer the most fundamental question faced by every congregation, "What does God want us to do and to be?" As we brainstormed in groups, the air was filled with the squeak of markers as page after page of newsprint was taped to the walls and filled with ideas. Some ideas were very cautious, others verged on audacious, a few were even slightly crazy. There was a lot of laughter, and even some tears, for this was a group that had become used to being together to share thoughts that we may never have dared to verbalize before.

At the end of the day, our visioning process had crystallized into eleven proposals. Further refinement trimmed this number down to four — one for each window of opportunity. Most impressively, no fewer than 46 people had volunteered to do further work on their proposals!

Patterns of growth and decline

Such enthusiasm had not always been the case at Scarboro United. Like many established churches, Scarboro has experienced a number of peaks and valleys. Periods of rapid growth, expansion of facilities, and program development seemed inevitably to have been followed by periods of retrenchment and relative inactivity.

The history of Scarboro United Church can be traced back to 1908 — a mere 14 years after the official birth of the city of Calgary. In that year, the first service of Bankview Methodist Church was held in the home of Mr. and Mrs. P. Withel. The church was one of four preaching appointments of the Springbank Methodist Mission. In 1909, a new home for the church was dedicated, and in 1920 its name was changed to Scarboro Methodist.

Also in 1908, Bankview Presbyterian Church was organized as both church and school house. This building was enlarged several times as the congregation grew.

On June 10, 1925, Scarboro Methodist and Bankview Presbyterian both joined The United Church of Canada. In September, 1927, these two congregations became one as Bankview Scarboro United. Worship services were held in the Presbyterian building. In 1929, the new unified congregation had a new home with the dedication of Scarboro Avenue United Church.

During the 1930's and 1940's, Scarboro was the religious and social focus of a growing urban community. Couples' clubs and numerous social activities flourished during hard economic times. In 1945, the manse was built and, in 1947, the mortgage was burned. During the postwar boom, growth in church membership was rapid. In 1951, the church was enlarged and the Memorial Hall, including a gymnasium, was built. In 1957, an additional extension to the church was added, and a small chapel was constructed.

But during the 1960s and 1970s, Scarboro United suffered the same fate as many other churches across Canada. Church ceased to be the social and religious focal point of family life. Youth groups, once healthy and active, no longer attracted teenagers, and Sunday school enrollment began to decline. By the early 1970s church attendance began to fall. Congregation members did not pick up their share of the work. The minister was, in effect, expected to be Chairman of the Christian Education Committee, Superintendent of the Sunday school, Co-ordinator of midweek groups, and Chair of the Official Board in addition to the usual pastoral duties of preaching, counselling, and visiting. Many programs were dropped, and it became increasingly difficult to handle the work of the church.

Developing a global outreach perspective

In 1973, a group of concerned church members met and, calling themselves the March 11 Committee, issued a wake-up call for change. The result of this group's encouragement was a major overhaul of the church's organizational structure. Functional committees were established with regularly scheduled meetings. The somewhat old unwieldy board organization was replaced with a more streamlined, effective operation.

Having established a more effective way to run its affairs, Scarboro church entered a new phase of its development. Church membership stabilized in the mid '70s. The late 1970s and 1980s saw an increase in a number of committee initiatives, particularly in the area of outreach. A joint initiative with Sacred Heart, a nearby Catholic Church, resulted in the construction of Bankview House, an apartment building for senior citizens, with rent set individually at 25% of income. Administration of this building continues to be shared by the two churches. Substantial fund-raising initiatives were also undertaken for women's shelters, in addition to regular drives for the Inter-faith Food Bank. Of course, we supported fully the United Church's Mission and Service Fund, averaging over the nine years a $27,000 yearly contribution.

But as early as 1985, some members expressed a desire to become more closely involved in outreach projects where we could more directly know what our money was accomplishing.

Consequently, in the summer of 1985, our part-time assistant minister urged us to participate in a project in Kenya. He himself went to Lodwar, Kenya to help dig wells. He took $1135 raised from the congregation to assist with the project.

But it wasn't until 1986 when we met Paul Carrick of CAUSE Canada that we became more fully involved in Third World development projects. CAUSE (the acronym stands for Christian Assistance for Underdeveloped Societies Everywhere) is a non-governmental organization committed to assisting the destitute and impoverished people of the world — not only by helping people to help themselves, but also by educating people about the real causes of and solutions for mass poverty. Specifically, CAUSE seeks to implement self-help projects in association with local churches of the developed world. Individual congregations are encouraged to provide financial support for specific development projects as well as to involve their members as overseas volunteers. Money raised by individual churches is often matched by provincial and/or federal grants.

Scarboro members became involved first in a 1986-88 medical project in Todos Santos, Guatemala, Central America. This district in the northeast part of the country had a population of about 15,000 indigenous people, with no medical facilities or assistance within several hundred miles. Money raised by Scarboro (and matched by grants) renovated an existing building to become a well-equipped medical clinic and also provided training for a local man as a health worker. The clinic has been operating since 1988. It is self-supporting and now has a Guatemalan physician in attendance four months of the year as well as the health worker and a full-time nurse.

In 1989 we accepted a second project with CAUSE Canada — this one in Ganta, Liberia. The new project was to educate villagers about sanitation, to help build latrines and water wells, to train and supervise village health workers, and to continue an immunization program . Scarboro's commitment and contribution was approximately $7,000 in cash with a further $3,000 that financed a volunteer from the congregation to work in Liberia for four months. Though political problems in

Liberia interrupted this project, and some of the money raised went instead to a similar project in Sierra Leone, Scarboro members made a third two-year commitment in 1991-92 to a CAUSE project.

This third project was again located in Todos Santos, Guatemala. Clean water was available to most villages only by having women and children carry it from distances of one to four kilometres. The villagers asked for assistance in building conduits from fresh water sources in the mountains to pipe water directly to the villages. In conjunction with the piped water, CAUSE provided a health education program. Scarboro raised $11,000, which was further matched by government agencies. Two members of our congregation spent time in 1991 in Todos Santos, one for two months, working with the health education program.

Scarboro United continued with yet another project in Todos Santos, this time the Women's Assistance Program. We committed ourselves to raising $10,000 to teach women health, literacy, and nutrition; to give them experience in designing and implementing community projects; and to promote gender sensitivity in the communities. In all there are a total of 25 projects in 15 target villages.

A need for a new vision

With the dawning of the 1990s, financial support for individual initiatives such as CAUSE Canada was strong, but it was not matched by a commitment to volunteering time and involvement in local issues.

Many church members were active in the community, but the congregation as a whole seemed to lack a sense of purpose. Opportunities to come together as a church family were largely limited to the social time after the worship service and to occasional potluck suppers. We worried about how to integrate newcomers into our midst, how to involve them in the work of the church, and how to inspire them with some of the opportunities for service.

We were also increasingly aware of our church's close proximity to Calgary's downtown area. The recession that hit Calgary in the early '80s was immediately followed by a national economic downturn. Unemployment rose. The number of street people increased. The church was more frequently asked for help by people in desperate need.

It was at this crucial point that our church was invited to join in a congregational vitalization program initiated and provided by the Vancouver School of Theology. Our decision to be involved was somewhat grudging at first. The program required a major investment of time spread over a year and a half and potentially involved a huge number of people.

We were concerned that our minister might find the additional workload too burdensome. We worried about sustaining interest and motivating our members to participate.

The vitalization program was formally initiated in October 1990. We chose to call the program "VIVA" (Vitally Inspired, Vitally Alive).

Discovering ourselves

Phase I of the program involved a review of the history of the congregation — the events that formed us, the decisions that defined us, the times that shaped us and the themes that described us. We chose to implement this phase in our congregation by holding one hour meetings on four Sundays, immediately following the worship service. Attendance was loosely arranged so as to have people who joined Scarboro before 1960 at the first meeting, then people who came in the 1960s, 1970s and 1980s, respectively, at subsequent meetings. Our idea was that by having peer groups we would jog each other's memory about significant events in our history. In a small group setting people were encouraged to relate these significant memories and to reflect on the importance of our past. Official "scribes" consolidated and published a report.

The process reminded us of our roots and our core values. It helped us realize that any successful move towards change must take these factors into account. We discovered that our history has, for the most part, been marked by quiet change and evolution rather than cataclysmic turning points. We have always been a "traditional" congregation — valuing the fundamentals of our faith, honouring the worship service as the central activity in our church life, and embracing "family" values of friendship, caring, and intergenerational relationships. Our desire to stay together as a cohesive group has sometimes led us to minimize divisive issues so as to avoid open confrontation. We have made many changes in our congregational life but always within a context of practical accommodation. We respect the past and have never rushed into change for the sake of change. We have a history of managing our finances in a prudent way. Our church buildings have been maintained in good condition and are a source of pride and inspiration to many of the congregation.

Equally significantly, perhaps, we realized that while Scarboro has always fostered a sense of mission, we have rarely been involved in supporting broad issues or causes. We have tended to support individual initiatives, particularly by funding a short-term cause that appeals to us, rather than by making an on-going commitment of volunteer time.

Phase II of the vitalization process caused us to focus our attention on the present — to examine the size and characteristics of our congregation (approximately 300 households and 200 financial supporters), and to itemize our programs and resources. This phase also called for an analysis of the communities we serve including an exploration of opportunities for new or expanded ministry.

We discovered some interesting facts about our congregation:

- Education: 72% of members have at least one university degree,
- Occupation: 71% are professional or retired,
- Gender: 65% are female,
- Children: 73% of households have no children under 20,
- Youth: 5 % of households have teenagers,
- Income: 60% of households have an annual income of over $45,000,
- Single Parents: 1% of households have a single parent,
- Age: 42% are between 30-39, and 42% are over 60,
- Proximity: 87% live within a 15 minute drive of the church.

This profile differs significantly from the demographics of the communities on our doorstep. Specifically, we are older, have more education, are better employed, are less ethnically diverse, have fewer children, earn more, and are less likely to be separated or divorced. Scarboro is in an affluent, well-established neighbourhood of single family homes on the fringes of downtown. The adjacent communities of Sunalta, Connaught, and Bankview are more densely populated, and more transient.

Losing a comfortable equilibrium

Following the publication of Phase II data, many of our members expressed unease at the disparity between the make-up of our membership and the nature of the communities we seek to serve. Concern was also expressed over the lack of young people in our church. These feelings carried forward into Phase III, the theological component of the vitalization program. The book *Of Bodies, Priests and Stewards* by Bud Phillips (published by the Vancouver School of Theology for this course) helped us focus our discussion. At Scarboro, we compressed the suggested eight-session series into six sessions, offered on Sundays after church and also on Thursday evenings and on Saturdays. A total of 103 people participated in the sessions; thirteen of our members acted as group facilitators.

Phase III encouraged us not only to reflect on our theology but to consider the practical implications of our beliefs. For example, participants considered the concept of the church as a haven in a heartless world.

We then considered whether Scarboro could be described in this way. We concluded that while Scarboro is a place of fellowship, solace, nurturing and spiritual renewal for its members, it does not serve the same purpose for the surrounding community.

Another session focused on the consideration of two continua:

- Preservation thinking ("looking after our own") vs. Service thinking ("open door attitude"), and
- Maintenance activities ("maintaining church programs and resources") vs. Mission activities ("putting theology into action outside the church").

Participants clearly indicated that Scarboro leaned towards preservation thinking and maintenance activities. As the Phase III sessions continued, it became apparent that there was a gap between what we as a congregation felt called to do and be, and the reality of our situation. We increasingly saw that gap as our window of opportunity.

Visioning Day was the culmination of the Phase III process. Armed with the knowledge of our historical context, our present reality, and our theological beliefs, we were able to propose some exciting courses of action for our church to explore. Of the four proposals carried forward, only two actually made it to Phase V, the implementation stage. None of us, however, think of this as failure. The two projects that are up and running — our Outreach program, serving Connaught Community School, and our GIFT Committee (Growing In Faith Together), which is dedicated to innovative approaches to adult Christian education — both serve as a positive contribution to our surrounding community and have greatly enriched our congregational life.

Working with Connaught school and community

The Connaught project involves an inner-city school about eight blocks from the church. We had discovered that we were well educated (72% had at least one university degree), that we had a number of retired members (in other words, many were not restricted by an 8-5 job), and that our income was above average (60% of households earned over $45,000). We had financed numerous outreach programs to other countries. But what about using our hands-on resources? Were we ready to? Many of the congregation were content with the status quo. Others felt that the congregation lacked an awareness of the volunteer opportunities available in our community. That Visioning Day in April 1991 included a number of teachers among the participants. Perhaps their participation led to a suggestion to find ways of working with the support system already in place at Connaught Community School. The proposal would cover special-needs areas of illiteracy, social isolation of parents, economic hardship, as well as single-parent and immigrant families.

Connaught is a special-needs community school. It differs from an ordinary elementary school in having a special mandate to work closely with parents, community groups, and community agencies to make the school the focal point in the area. Located in the Beltline inner-city area of Calgary, Connaught has a concentrated immigrant population because many of the newly arrived refugees and immigrants settle within walking distance of the school for at least their first year in Calgary. Both because of its proximity to us and its nature, Connaught was therefore a good place for Scarboro volunteers to begin.

Our proposal was to actively support four existing programs at the school — a toy lending library for Connaught and community children, a literacy program, the family resource centre, and an Immigrant Buddy program.

We approached the school administration and were received warmly. Most schools have parent help and Connaught is no exception. But often these parents are unable to help in the classrooms with the actual coaching of the students because they can't speak fluent English.

By October 1991, a crew of 20 volunteers began work. Some helped students, in classes and individually, with reading, writing, science, and mathematics; some shelved books in the library; some staffed the toy-lending library at various hours; some assisted in the office. Two years later, we are still volunteering in any way we can. There is more need than ever for individual help with ESL students (English as a second language), and volunteers with computer knowledge are popular. We still have about 16 regular weekly volunteers working at whatever jobs we are asked to fill.

We have tried to help Connaught in other ways, too. For two years now, we have asked that gifts for our White Gift Sunday be new toys to help replenish those at the Connaught Lending Library. We have helped to cover the costs of an extra-curricular swim program for which the parents of students often cannot afford to pay. We have contributed items of used clothing to the tables that the school keeps filled for families who need extra apparel. Adele Zanutig, Connaught's Community School Coordinator, said recently, "Involving volunteers from Scarboro United Church in the total education process of our school has helped develop quality education. As we endeavor to meet the diverse needs of our student population, Scarboro volunteers who listen to students read, assist in the library, tutor students and share their many talents are an invaluable help to both Connaught Community School and the Connaught Community."

In 1992, we decided to join the City of Calgary's Adopt-a-Family Christmas project, focusing particularly on families from Connaught School who needed help. (We had done some Christmas Hampers since 1989 — more loosely organized at first, simply helping families from two or three schools where we knew principals or teachers.) After becoming involved in Connaught School, we had 39 individuals or groups from the church respond to the need, "adopting" 39 families. This experience reinforced our volunteer program at the school. At least one "adopting" member decided to become a regular volunteer, based on her experience with the family she met when she delivered the food and gifts.

When Calgary's Social Services department, which had been struggling with the organization and distribution of Christmas assistance for poverty-stricken families, decided in 1993 that it hadn't the human resources or time to continue, Scarboro Church was quick to fill the gap. Led by two volunteer co-cordinators from our church and a City of Calgary employee, a computer database program was set up to organize distribution. Scarboro volunteers entered data submitted by the city's social workers, to find and register groups and individuals who would "adopt " families. There were many phone calls to set up drop-offs and pick-ups of the hampers and many hours spent to record all details in the computer. To distribute 310 hampers (about 1800 cartons of food and presents), a two-day army of Scarboro volunteers had the satisfaction of bringing joy to many of Calgary's needy.

One of the most heart-warming moments was a small boy's delight when he saw that part of his family's hamper was a two-wheeled bicycle with his name on it. His reaction brought tears to the eyes of a number of workers. In all, about 40 Scarboro workers helped make the Adopt-a-Family hamper project a success.

The following year, Scarboro took over full responsibility for the project from the city's Social Services Department.

The original proposal had included an Immigrant Family Buddy Program, but we had decided in the first year of the Connaught project that we would concentrate on the school program. In 1992, however, we approached the Calgary Catholic Immigration Society Host Program to have a representative speak one morning at church to explain the responsibilities of hosting an immigrant family. From this invitation came our first volunteer host for two newly arrived Bosnian families. Though only one Scarboro member was the host, many others helped to supply furniture, clothing and other special needs. By 1994, another congregation family was hosting a third Bosnian family.

Growing in Faith Together

The second project that emerged from our vitalization program was the GIFT Committee, established in the fall of 1991 to provide family and adult programs in three areas:
- Church rituals, history and structure
- Bible study
- Family life

Because we had learned during the VIVA process that Sunday after church service was our best time to meet, most of our programs begin about noon after a quick bag lunch and finish between 2:00 and 2:30 p.m. Each program has followed a similar format — an opening presentation (a guest speaker, film strips, a video, a workshop leader), then an opportunity to join small groups to answer questions, share reactions, and discuss feelings.

The GIFT committee has responded to specific requests received from the congregation. A variety of topics have been included so far:
- Advent
- Baptism
- Communion
- Aboriginal Spirituality
- Overcoming Grief and Loss
- Bible Overview, which led in turn to a weekly Bible study
- *Jesus Then and Now* (ed. David Watson et al, Lion USA, 1987) — a six-week Lenten Bible study
- *Unplug the Christmas Machine* (Jo Robinson and Jean Coppock Staeheli, William Morrow, New York, 1991) — offered two consecutive years

Attendance at GIFT presentations has been gratifying, ranging from 30 to over 70. Recently the programs have been advertised in community newspapers in the area and there has been some initial response. We hope that as the community becomes more aware of what is offered, we will get further response.

Interest has been expressed in learning about other faiths too. The committee has presented two programs of information on other faiths, interspersing them with programs about our own faith. One Friday evening about 50 members from our congregation and neighbouring St. Matthew's United Church, guided by Mr. Herkirat Singh, toured the Sikh *gurdwara* (church) and learned about the history of the Sikh faith. Another night, at our own church, about 100 people attended a Seder dinner, a festive family liturgy/meal that Jewish people celebrate on the first two nights of Passover. Rabbi Roy Tanenbaum and Loretta Tanenbaum guided us through the Seder liturgy. The Passover story was told in a question and answer format, with special emphasis on teaching the children.

A two-Sunday intergenerational session included a tour of our own church building with knowledgeable individuals stationed at specific points of historical interest. A second session allowed members to share memories of their life in the church. The goal of these sessions was to learn more about each other while crossing intergenerational barriers in the process.

Because the committee prepares three or four programs a year, twelve members work in small groups of two or three to plan. The whole committee meets to evaluate past presentations and to make plans for future ones.

The many hopes, ideas and dreams that began over two years ago have meant hard work, some mistakes, and much enjoyment for committee members. It has been a learn-by-doing experience. For the members of the congregation, the GIFT committee has helped us to develop a real awareness of the opportunities for individual and collective spiritual growth.

A revitalized community of Christians

Perhaps more important than the external actions is the ongoing effect of our church's participation in a vitalization program. It has taught us to stop taking church membership for granted. For many of us it was the first time we ever thought of setting goals for our church, the first time we had challenged ourselves to make a difference, the first time we had not accepted the status quo.

It is also satisfying for us to reflect that many new committee initiatives may be traced, directly or indirectly, to the vitalization process. We began our focus on Connaught School because we saw a special need. But from this association we have developed an awareness far beyond what we originally perceived.

We were interested in a new sense of direction and a new sense of purpose, and we are finding that direction and purpose continually broadening and deepening. We feel a greater sense of our city — the cultural mix, the needs that exist amongst those less fortunate, and the role we can play in meeting those needs.

We wanted to be more involved in the welfare of the homeless. We have since increased our support of CUPS (Calgary Urban Project Society — an agency offering medical assistance and other help to street people) and we organized, financed and served a dinner for 300 people at The Mustard Seed, a downtown social ministry.

We expressed our desire to be more accessible. We have built ramps, installed an elevator, and renovated the washrooms for people with disabilities.

We expressed the need to study our Christian faith. We have developed programs to enhance our knowledge of the Bible, of other religions, and of the structure of our church.

We expressed our concern about the lack of young people in our church. We now have two Youth Groups, plus an ever-increasing Sunday school enrollment. And we look forward to greater involvement of our young people, for we have recently hired a part time commissioned minister to focus on Christian Development work. The need for more programs for our children and youth and for the staff to carry out those programs was clearly articulated through the VIVA project.

The initiatives we take now tend to be more "risky," both financially and in terms of volunteer commitment, than those we might have chosen in the past. Certainly the church has undergone a change process. Have the faces we see in the congregation changed too? Yes, some have. And those that have not seem more familiar, for many of us know each other much better. The dreams of those 70 people gathered on that Visioning Day in April, 1991, have created new inspiration and life in Scarboro United Church.

Susan Murphy has been a member of Scarboro United since 1981 and presently serves as editor of The Uniter, a quarterly church newsletter. Married with two teenaged children, she is currently pursing a career as a freelance writer.

Enid Holtby is a retired English teacher and 30-year member of Scarborough United Church.

Inadequate facilities were holding St. Paul's United in Halifax back from fulfilling their goals of community service. With a new building came new opportunities.

6

Riding the renewal train

by MONA DRABBLE

The final straw was when Earl, Jim, and Ron climbed down the ladder gruffly proclaiming, "That's the last time I'll tar that roof!"

Then the rains fell. We waded through puddles and tripped over drip-buckets standing sullenly about the gym floor. Meetings all moved to our tiny lower hall. We peeked around posts. Youth groups switched to quiet games to avoid injury. The cramped nursery had no windows and was continually overheating. Our Christian Development Committee was totally discouraged with the inadequate space and lack of ways to separate the Sunday school classes. The building was developing severe structural flaws, and the plumbing was leaking in the washroom.

At the same time, our area on the east side of Halifax was growing. It had been a rural area outside Halifax until the 1950s. It became a working class, low income area. Although the number of people in our congregation was not increasing, the needs of people in the community were. What we wanted to do simply could not be done in our old building.

Squeezed between a rock and a hard place

The adjoining shopping mall brought steady foot traffic past our church day and night. Not all of them felt protective about the church. After the second theft of our computer and office equipment, with broken windows and doors that had to be repaired, our patience was wearing thin.

The congregation made a decision to sell and rebuild. Unfortunately, the decision of the United Church's General Council, meeting in Victoria that summer (1988), that homosexual persons could be considered for ordination, resulted in a lot of local controversy and a drop in membership. But we proceeded, despite cautions from our pastor.

A warm-hearted, strikingly generous offer of roughly four acres of land offered a way out, and the land was purchased from the province. We were underway. The mall developers bought the old church and demolished it. We watched it fall through falling tears, but we were already aboard our building train and there was no turning back.

The summer of 1989 we held church services in the local Junior High School under the direction of the Rev. Donald MacLeod, a delightfully Scottish retired minister. Our former pastor, John Moses, had accepted a call to Ontario. The inconvenience of our temporary meeting-place was sweetened by the refreshments served after every service by Desi and Karen Ettinger. We lingered, ate, and planned.

In January of 1989 we engaged a stewardship consultant, to guide us through a campaign with the theme, "Our future is now." The campaign proved very successful.

Choosing a ready-made design

A building committee was formed, with Pat Connors as chair, and architects interviewed. We chose Chapelstone, Inc. They had good designs, were well organized where fees and costs were concerned, and had built 27 churches in the Maritimes in the past year. Their total fee was $45,000. We think we saved $160,000 by going with a "design-built" company.

Chapelstone produced preliminary plans and studies. The congregation was consulted every step of the way. We had lofty dreams but, in the end, we had to shelve our plans for a seniors' complex and a daycare. We simply did not have the funds to carry out all our dreams.

We studied the plans for Carleton Kirk United Church in Saint John, N.B., and liked the friendly semi-circular seating arrangement of their sanctuary. We visited two other churches in our area built by "our" architect, and were impressed by their simple beauty, convenience, comfort and good size.

We chose our design. We placed the fellowship hall downstairs, with folding doors between the Sunday school rooms. There was space on that floor for our food bank, the outreach office, the church office, the minister's study and a "dream" kitchen for the women's groups that featured a commercial quality dishwasher and fridge, a floating centre island, and beautiful cupboards.

Upstairs the sanctuary featured movable furniture for the choir, which meant the chancel platform could be used in many ways. The faithful had requested a roomy foyer, and there was storage space behind the chancel for bell choir equipment. There are two over-flow areas for seating, one of which is used by the UCW as "their meeting parlour." The other has dual use, either as sanctuary seating or as a board room. The building is wheelchair accessible with a small elevator for use by the elderly or people with disabilities. We can seat a total of 200 people in the sanctuary, 40 in the board room and 65 in the parlour — a grand total of 305. We use it all at Christmas and Easter, and for some funerals or weddings.

Basically, our two-storey design encompassed facilities for ministry to the congregation, for Christian development, and for our outreach ministry.

Sod was broken on a dark and rainy Sunday afternoon, June 18, 1989, by the oldest and the youngest church members. Not one word was raised in complaint against the weather, just ringing voices singing "The Church's One Foundation." Our motto was, "The bitterness of poor quality remains long after the sweetness of low price has disappeared." Our standing joke was, "Never has so much been accomplished by so few with so little."

At first our new church was just a jungle of metal supports. The clutter might have intimidated the eye, but it was a comfort to our hearts to see that strong steel going up. Now we realized how the building would fit into the hillside, but it was still difficult to picture the finished structure until the walls were added.

The new church was opened in March of 1990.

New possibilities for service programs

Having a building allowed us to carry on our community outreach program. We call it the Family Resources Institute. St. Paul's wanted to develop an agency capable of responding to the needs of the com-

munity. The importance of adapting to the new and ever-changing demands of society and responding appropriately to those demands was
a key point for us. The Long Range Planning Committee visualized an
agency that would discourage further dependence on social programs,
an agency that was rehabilitating rather than debilitating. The Institute would become a "resource developer" rather than a "service" provider. Its philosophy is simple: self-help and "the ability of people to
recognize that, despite their poverty, they have the power within themselves to change their lives and their circumstances."

The Institute was incorporated on September 18, 1985, and continued after reorganizing in the new building. In the interval, the food
bank operated out of local Emmanuel Anglican Church and the Continuing Education program from St. Michael's Roman Catholic Church.
Wonderful community co-operation is truly a blessing.

The Institute has a salaried co-ordinator, who has recently taken a
counselling course through university extension to be better able to
help people cope with their problems. It is about people helping people, creating an environment where self-actualization can be activated
and maintained. It is meant to help those who are disadvantaged or at
risk of becoming so.

This year our programs include the food bank and an adult upgrading education program with a baby-sitting service. We give a bo-
nus to our food bank overseer, once a consumer but now its supervisor.
The education upgrading program is staffed by a fully qualified, very
dedicated and hard-working teacher certified by the Department of
Education.

In addition, we present a low-cost cooking program, also with a
sitter service. And we thrilled to our first community garden this year.
"My bit of paradise," one gardener described it. We had a part-time
paid co-ordinator for that. We now have a grant to run an educational
program teaching parenting skills with difficult teens. The local community service centre provided a director.

Our philosophy is to initiate programs and then try to have them
taken over and continued by community agencies. A good example is
our nationally acclaimed prenatal program. This began with a grant
from Health Canada and evolved into a Single Parent Centre funded
by the Home of the Guardian Angel, a private, non-profit community
agency.

Our clothing bank joined those of the other local churches and has
been centrally located in a community facility. It is funded by the St.
Vincent de Paul Society as an ecumenical service and is staffed by
volunteers from all the local churches and by consumers.

A food bank, plus

Our Food Bank co-ordinator, Heather Coffin, recently conducted and recorded a needs assessment. Her recommendation was that our goal should be "to work with and to gain input from the consumers of the food bank in developing a program that will improve the life skills of people living in poverty in the community." A number of projects have emerged from this.

Heather now publishes and distributes a monthly newsletter to the four food banks in our area. This dispenses information to our consumers highlighting nutrition, budget suggestions, and low cost recipes. It lists community programs — job programs, information about the provincial family benefits program, single parent support, etc.

We provide an employment board. where people can examine current job listings from the Canada Employment and Immigration Centre. We are also associated with the "Inner City Grassroots Grocery Organization." Consumers may purchase meat orders at wholesale prices from this non-profit neighbourhood grocery store.

Our food bank is always an active spot in the church. People go away not just with food but with helpful advice, enjoyable budget recipes, and most important of all, with a smile on their faces.

At Christmas last year the St. Paul's Family Resources Institute aided 87 families with a turkey, a carton of groceries, mittens and toys for the children. Sambro United Church holds a "mitten tree" for us by decorating a twig tree with all the colourful mittens in all sizes that are knitted by volunteers. When the tree is full the mittens are sent to add to the Christmas parcels. Local schools also organize toy drives to furnish the toys for this project.

The future is packed with challenges, but with God's help and guidance, we will meet them all.

Mona Drabble is secretary of the Unified Board of St. Paul's, chair of the Concerned Visitation Committee and a director of the Family Resources Institute. She has been involved for 27 years in the Scouting and Guiding movement as a leader, commissioner and District Council President. She has also volunteered as a director of the Community Services Centre, Sunday school teacher and superintendent, and UCW quilter, among other things.

The amalgamation of two struggling congregations in North Vancouver, which might be seen as an act of defiance to an increasingly secular and privatized world, led to renewed vitality for Deep Cove and Mount Seymour United churches.

7

Living
the story

by BRIAN THORPE

As the congregation began to arrive on a winter Sunday in early 1989 for their weekly worship service in the Seycove Community School gym, they sensed a startling difference. The now-familiar incense of mouldy gym sock had been replaced by the pungency of stale beer. Slightly deflated balloons bounced against the ceiling.

The place was a mess. A fund-raising casino held by the school the night before had left its mark.

The congregation, by this time accustomed to such surprises, took the new environment in its stride. They set up stacking chairs. They brought in the worship resources that lived, for six months, in the back of the Hodgsons' station wagon. The choir assembled in the band room; the Sunday school teachers created their makeshift classrooms.

As the processional hymn began on the portable organ, I suddenly realized the choir and worship leaders were not processing on dry ground at all, but were, in fact, sloshing through pools of spilled beer.

I remember wondering what our Methodist forebears would have thought of us.

The story of an amalgamation

That Sunday morning marked the midway point of our journey. The Deep Cove and Mount Seymour United churches had begun an exciting venture in 1982. After many years of shared ministry, these two congregations at either end of the Seymour area in North Vancouver had decided to create a new future together.

Deep Cove had the longer history. It had begun in 1937, to serve a somewhat isolated little resort community on Indian Arm of Burrard Inlet. After a number of years of meeting in the Dance Pavilion and the Fire Hall, they built a church on a piece of land purchased for $150. (Thirty-five years later, the land for the new church would cost $450,000.)

During this time, the congregation was served by a series of theological students and retired supplies. When they eventually did get a full-time minister, in the 1960s, he was shared with Seymour Heights (later Mount Seymour) and Lynmour United churches.

The Seymour Heights/Mount Seymour congregation also got started in the 1930s. Like Deep Cove, they rented quarters in the community hall for many years. In 1959, a church home was opened on Berkley Road. It was, literally, a home — a large ranch-style house provided a manse for the minister on the top floor, with the sanctuary located below in what would normally be the recreation room. A converted carport served as office, meeting room, choir room, and congregational library. The Sunday school and pre-school met in a portable classroom.

But by the 1980s, dramatic changes were taking place in the community served by these two small congregations. A new bridge across the Seymour River prompted a rapid increase in population, from 11,000 to over 20,000 people. Projections by the District of North Vancouver forecast 30,000 to 40,000 people before long.

In Deep Cove, 3,000 square foot homes were replacing the former randomly placed recreational cottages. Between Deep Cove and Seymour Heights, a whole new community of young families was emerging.

In February 1982, the Annual Meetings of the two congregations (Lynmour had ceased to exist in 1967) passed a resolution to "explore different ways the two congregations could work together in the immediate and longer term future." This resolution was followed by four years of surveys, congregational meetings, tours of other churches, conversations with architects and with Presbytery and civic governments.

The culmination of these years of creative labour was the production of a mission design for the congregation. Brad Newcombe, the minister during this period, describes marathon writing sessions for the mission design that went on well into the night. The imaginations of several key members of the congregation were fuelled by the excitement of developing a new style of ministry for this developing area.

In 1986, the Deep Cove church was sold. This was one of the most difficult steps of the whole process. Unlike the Mount Seymour building — which was never intended to be anything but an interim home — the Deep Cove church had the look and feel of a long established rural church. Indeed, its country *ambiance* had made it popular for smaller weddings. The congregation's attachment to this sanctuary was strong.

The final service in Deep Cove, which occurred four months after my arrival in the pastoral charge, showed a whole range of mixed emotions. The excitement of the new venture and the lament of saying farewell to an old friend mingled in the liturgy.

Coping creatively with controversies

After holding two services every Sunday in the Mount Seymour church, this building was also sold in 1988. Its final service came the Sunday immediately following the closing of probably the most divisive General Council in the history of The United Church of Canada.

I had been a commissioner in Victoria for that Council. The contrast between the apprehensive mood of the closing of Council and the celebrative tone at Mount Seymour was striking. A new challenge quickly puts the political conflicts of a denomination into perspective.

Mount Seymour's response to the conflict racking the United Church was to hold a September sermon series, followed by three well-attended study sessions. Differences that surfaced were handled by the congregation with care, compassion and love.

This experience foreshadowed the way in which the congregation(s) would talk through their own controversies, as we began the process of building a new community together. If we could live with the tensions around sexual orientation and ministry, we could handle the more contentious issue of whether to have pews or chairs in our new sanctuary!

Complex negotiations with the District of North Vancouver caused delays. For six months, we had to make a temporary home in the local high school. That was where we baptized our feet with beer. The church office moved to the basement of my home.

There was some nervousness about this phase in the journey. A worst case scenario imagined people staying away in droves. After all, the argument went, who would want to worship in a gym? A great many people, apparently. During our first two months in the gym, we welcomed over 20 new families into the congregation.

As we reflected on this phenomenon, we realized that two things were happening. First, we were together as a congregation at last. We no longer had to cope with the dissipation of energy that comes from living in two locations or holding two services. Second, we were accessible in a way that traditional sanctuaries often are not. We were the centre of things, in an informal, non-threatening, community school.

Meanwhile, on the construction site

While we were meeting in the school, the building program was in full gear. Several important things were put in place by the congregation to ensure that the stress of building would not overwhelm their creativity.

The New Church Development Committee, under the leadership of Ted Butterfield, developed a structure that encouraged people to contribute what they could to particular aspects of the program, while allowing them to come and go as personal agendas required.

Jim Roberts, who was chair of the Board and had particular skills in landscaping and building design, took on the often frustrating role of negotiating, on an almost daily basis, with the District of North Vancouver on issues of land purchase, zoning of the old property, building design and location. At a critical point in the process, we actually had to turn the whole building around.

We made a decision to be realistic about congregational participation in the actual building process. We were aware of the potential costs of undoing the mistakes made by well-meaning amateurs. At the same time, we also knew how important it could be to offer hands-on experience, to help the congregation feel real ownership of this project. We felt that the best way to do this was to commit volunteer labour to interior painting — everything except the sanctuary. And indeed our painting sessions proved to be exciting community-building events.

But the most important dynamic during this period had nothing to do with the building. The leadership of the congregation had decided that it was essential, during the building program, to maintain and build the community of faith. They played out this conviction by calling a minister (myself) who did not want to be actively involved either driving a bulldozer or running a financial campaign. I kept in touch with what was going on, but I devoted most of my energy to worship leadership, adult study, and pastoral work. That division of labour was mirrored in the congregation: some folk devoted most of their volunteer time to the building project; others taught Sunday school, maintained the mission and outreach network, and cared for members in need.

By the spring of 1989 we were ready for the opening celebration. We had planned it for the last Sunday in April. At things turned out, we had actually been in the building for a couple of previous Sundays.

The realities of pastoral care

Our first service in the building was a memorial service. A few months before, while we were still meeting in the gym, Raymonde had risen spontaneously to tell the congregation of her terminal illness. While the final stages of construction and interior finishing were taking place, a small group of other members had engaged in a ministry of prayer and presence with Raymonde. So it seemed appropriate that the labour of hand and heart could be celebrated together in our first act of worship in the new building.

The first Sunday worship was on Easter Sunday. At 4:00 that morning, I typed the last page of a PhD thesis. Through several years of extended study leaves, its completion had eluded me. In the end, it was finished not in the comparative calm of private study, but in the frantic bustle of church-building, congregational growth, and the busiest time in the liturgical calendar.

Walking to the new church that Easter Sunday, I realized in a new way that new life rarely emerges from placid circumstances. The risks of building, the demand for flexibility during our time of dislocation, the call to create a vibrant Christian community in a highly secular environment — all these combined to create a climate in which human energy and creativity flourished.

We had built a church and much more. As I learned about the lives of others in the community, I realized that my experience of renewed vigour was not an isolated incident.

This shouldn't be surprising. Risk and chaos have always been the nurturing ground for resurrection.

Celebrating with silence

Shortly after Easter, the Sunday for dedicating our new home arrived. We had decided to begin the day with a "clown communion" at our regular worship time. Despite a few misgivings, it proved to be a memorable service. After years of words and more words, some of them quite argumentative, many of them tinged with weariness and frustration, it felt appropriate to worship in the language of silence with the clowns. In this silence, we rehearsed the foundational story of our faith, we danced in the aisles, and we shared a common meal.

That afternoon, the Presbytery service of dedication took place. It was a low key, by-the-book, event. Five years later, few can remember much of that service. The real dedication, the one people remember, took place with the clowns, earlier that morning.

By that evening, the realities of life sank in. I lay down, to take what seemed to be a well-deserved rest. At that moment, two messages arrived. One told me that a member who had danced with the clowns that morning had died suddenly in the afternoon. And as this news sank in, Sheila Norris knocked on my door to tell me that the condominium complex just down the street from our new church was on fire.

Pastoral care for a family in grief, and opening up the church to homeless neighbours, showed that the day-to-day life of this newly housed Christian community had already begun.

When growth levels out

The first couple of years in the new building were a dynamic time. In numbers and spirit, we grew. Within two years, the congregation had doubled in size. So had the Sunday school. The Mission and Outreach Committee held evenings on Third World debt, on the impact of the Gulf War, on local poverty and violence. Several adult education events were arranged. We sponsored a Somalian family. We held annual retreats for men and for women. We had a monthly coffee house, with local bands playing. We opened a well-stocked church library. A thrift shop operated every Thursday. A pastoral care group known as FISH (Friends In Sharing and Helping) was formed.

Also, during these couple of years, the congregation raised over $30,000 through fund-raising events.

The congregation had always been characterized by good financial management. It needed to be, during this period. In 1985, before building started, the two congregations had a combined budget of $70,000, supported by about 100 active families. By 1990, there were 200 supporting families and a budget of $163,000.

Rapid growth began to slow in the third year after building. A few key families moved out of the area. We began to realize that escalating house prices made our area less affordable for the young families that our congregation suited so well. The recession had been slow in coming to British Columbia, but now unemployment hit several in our congregation.

And overriding all these factors was another that faces all New Church Development congregations sooner or later — the newness of our venture had begun to wear off. What had been exciting developments now settled down to be routine. Worship life and Sunday school felt competition from Sunday morning recreational programs in the surrounding community.

The congregation still seemed healthy, but there were more moments of lethargy than there had been.

Waiting too long to renew stewardship

This "plateau" in growth was felt most profoundly in our finances. By the beginning of the fourth year in the new building, 1993, givings had stagnated. They were even showing signs of decline. At the same time, the graduated payments due on our Ventures in Mission (VIM) loan continued to go up. It became apparent that a directed visitation of every person was in order.

There were some fears about our ability to mount such a campaign. Volunteer time had been diminishing, accompanying our financial woes.

But the fears were groundless. Once again the congregation rose to the occasion.

The visitation took place in the spring of 1993. The results were very encouraging, particularly in offers of service. We recorded over 1300 offers to serve in some capacity of the church's life. Pledges of financial giving in the church's life also showed an increase. The commitments made were not as high as the objective, but they were significant enough — an increase of 18% — to ease some of the feelings of financial pressure. The pressure was also eased by renegotiation of the VIM loan.

And by the fall of 1993, signs of renewed vigour could be noticed. Attendance at worship improved. Several new families became mainstays, within a few months of their arrival. One Sunday I encountered a woman who, in my mind, had been pretty much on the edge of the congregation. I saw she was carrying the Sunday school curriculum under her arm. I asked her if she were now teaching. I rather expected, with the jadedness that afflicts some of us who live in the church day after day, to hear her answer in tones reflecting a feeling of grudging duty. Instead, she replied with joy in her face and her voice: "Yes, and I'm just loving it!"

Such expressions of new life in the congregation seemed to grow as the fall went on.

Key factors that shaped the community

That November, I announced to the congregation that I would be leaving Mount Seymour in March, to become the Executive Secretary of B.C. Conference. The announcement precipitated the usual pastoral relations process. During it, we gave out a questionnaire to the congregation. They returned 150. The largest number of returns came from members in the 35-50 age bracket. This result offered statistical backing to a growing hunch that the congregation was entering a new phase in its ministry.

Much will be new in this next step along the way. Mount Seymour is now a well-established suburban congregation. The next phase will almost certainly involve a consolidation of programs and resources. It will be an important time of learning ways to challenge the rigidity that can grow in any established body. The gifts and challenges brought by new members will prove invaluable in this process.

Looking back, several factors shaped our community. And the lessons learned from the process of building a church and a faith community at the same time need to be kept before the community as it moves into the next stage of its growth.

As I see it, six foundational dynamics have undergirded this New Church Development.

1. Developing a broad understanding of stewardship

Early in the process of planning for the new church, the congregation realized the importance of building a base of giving. This giving did not focus on the building itself, but on the mission needs of the church in our community and beyond.

So the first major project at the time of New Church Development was a directed stewardship program. As Jim Roberts commented at the time: "We wanted members to get into the habit of giving to the local congregation *and* to Mission and Service before the bricks and mortar appeal started."

This initial appeal, in the early 1980s, had a highly successful result. Its value as an ongoing commitment of the congregation was demonstrated during the financial stresses when we hit that "plateau" in the early 1990s. Analysis showed us that one reason for the plateau was letting too many years pass before renewing the stewardship thrust that had launched the first period of growth.

So the program in 1993 was an important, if belated, recovery of the ongoing dynamic essential to congregational health.

2. Maintaining a focus on mission

One of the greatest dangers in building a church is the temptation to focus the spiritual life and work of the church inward. The history of Mount Seymour church reveals several deliberate moves to keep the congregation committed to the mission of the Christian community to a hurting world.

All along, the congregation has been blessed by an active Mission and Outreach Committee. Several members had a passion for acting on their Christian faith through local and global concerns. Through program and action, this committee kept concerns for ecological healing, peace, and just relationships before the congregation.

By contrast, the FISH (Friends In Sharing and Helping) group focused more on local needs. With the Mission and Outreach Committee, they maintained the congregation's commitment to First United Church, in Vancouver's downtown east side. Within the congregation, they created systems to respond to individual needs in the community. FISH also provided the initiative for the congregation's involvement in the ecumenical program Neighbourlink.

During the first year in the new building, Gladys Johnston and Jean Roberts shared their dream of a thrift shop. Establishing a weekly sale of good but used clothing was a bold venture. Four years later, it had grown to be an important part of the church program, involving several regular volunteers. In addition, it provided over $16,000 to the church treasury in 1993.

The Thrift Shop's outreach ministry has also been important. As in every affluent suburb, those in financial need may be more isolated than they would be in poorer neighbourhoods. The Thrift Shop opened the church to a wider community than that attracted by Sunday morning worship.

This sense of outward mission becomes more and more important as a congregation becomes established. It worked at Mount Seymour. Even the members themselves felt some pleasurable surprise at the financial statements for 1993. Although the congregation was barely holding its own on operational and building accounts, they had exceeded their goal for Mission and Outreach by 124%!

3. Celebrating along the way

Mount Seymour United Church is a congregation that likes to party. Its primary eschatological metaphor *must* be the great banquet! This too has been an important dynamic to maintain, especially during the sometimes tense and stressful times of church building:

- For the sod-turning in 1988, the congregation set up a parade, with a community band.
- Halfway through the building process, they held a Sunday lunch in the empty shell of what would eventually become their church.
- The opening of the new building was accompanied by a week of well-attended open houses.
- When a low rental housing project was completed next door to the church, the church hosted a week of lunches for the new neighbours in the midst of their moves.
- Silent auctions, "Guess Who's Coming to Dinner" events, and social evenings for newcomers, became part of the regular agenda of the church. "Guess Who's Coming to Dinner" is a fund-raiser/social event in which volunteer hosts entertain volunteer guests at dinner. A charge is made to all guests, which is paid to the church. Only the organizers know exactly who is going to dine in which home, until the guests actually arrive. It's a great way to get to know people!

One of the most controversial decisions related to celebration was whether or not to allow wine and beer to be served in the church hall. Many younger members, unfamiliar with the United Church's temperance legacy, couldn't understand what all the fuss was about.

It was one of those debates that had merit on both sides. On the one hand were those concerned about the highly addictive society in which we lived. They argued that the church should be a haven from the social pressures to drink. On the other hand were those who argued that, unless we made abstinence a requirement for Christian discipleship, it was hypocritical to engage in social drinking everywhere but in the church.

A vote by secret ballot made Mount Seymour one of the few United churches that allows — within certain restrictions — wine and beer to be served in its hall.

The congregation understood intuitively that it must not rely on Sunday worship alone to integrate people into the community. In the relaxed atmosphere of social events, people often discover that they are cared for, not only by God, but also by previously unknown neighbours in the pews.

4. Keeping the church open

Another important decision made during the time the church was being built was to gradually increase the hours worked by the church secretary, Betty Hodgson. They also expanded her role. Eventually, she became full-time church staff, with the title of "Church Co-ordinator." Betty's skill in office management and her pastoral sensitivity combine to make her an invaluable asset to the congregation. She keeps in touch with the church's network of volunteers, and often provides the first welcome to newcomers.

Having a full-time person in the office meant that the church could be open all day, every day. Combined with volunteers who keep the church open every weekday evening, this means that anyone coming to the church out of curiosity, or out of spiritual or physical need, rarely finds a locked door. And when people phone, they get a caring human voice, not a tape recording outlining highly restricted open hours.

The vision that prompted the building of Mount Seymour United Church included a desire to demonstrate a dynamic Christian presence in the community. It is costly for a congregation the size of Mount Seymour to have two full-time staff. But the message of the open church that is communicated to the community makes that cost more than worthwhile.

5. Telling the story

In today's culture, the Christian story is often an increasingly remote memory. Congregations can no longer base their worship and study life on assumptions of a common reservoir of knowledge of the Christian faith.

Some of the people who come through the doors of Mount Seymour carry with them the heritage of a strong United Church history. An increasing number, however, come from backgrounds in other faith traditions, or with no particular faith upbringing at all. Yet whatever their faith backgrounds, they all share a culture that is highly secularized. In surveys, the Vancouver area of British Columbia consistently reveals the lowest levels of church attendance anywhere in North America.

Mount Seymour sought to meet this challenge with a worship life that centres on earthy storytelling. Without the cultural props of socially-accepted Christendom, it seemed appropriate to go back to the roots of the Christian experience, in which the stories of the people of Israel and of Jesus' little band of disciples were told with a passion; a passion born out of the tellers' own experience that these encounters between God and humanity really do make a difference.

The emphasis on storytelling has been reflected in the preferred style of preaching. It is biblical, and it is passionate about the life issues faced by individuals and communities today.

It is also reflected in the music life of the congregation. One of the most significant areas of growth has been the choir. Donna Crook, who was the music director in Deep Cove United Church, and who continued that role in the new church, has nurtured a choir that has grown in membership and repertoire in the new building. There's no secret to this success, for everyone can see that joy and commitment with which the choir undertakes its ministry. The choir, in turn, reflects the ethos of the congregation with its steady commitment of time, its capacity to celebrate, and its concern that the music not only sound good but tell a real story.

Storytelling has also been important in Christian education. The Sunday school has been an important part of the life of the church. It has been nurtured by some highly committed folk — despite occasional frustrations at having to provide teachers in a mobile and busy community where few people can make long-term commitments.

More difficult has been the task of promoting adult education programs. The spirit may be willing, but the flesh is often overwhelmed by the frantic pace of contemporary middle-class life.

One of the most important issues confronting the congregation, in the years ahead, will be discovering ways in which the story of faith can be explored at greater depth than is possible in weekly worship settings.

6. Becoming fools for Christ

That first service, when the congregation opened its doors by inviting in the clowns, turns out to have continuing symbolic value.

Being the church is tough in today's world. We've all been hard hit by our loss of privileged position. No longer can we pressure local soccer or hockey leagues not to play on Sunday mornings, to assure ourselves of a captive market. In a culture obsessed with privatism, a culture increasingly cynical about historic institutions, the church's commitment to a historic faith and to the notion of community seems an anachronism. It makes the church seem out of touch, irrelevant. And the breakdown of a core of commonly held assumptions about faith and human identity can make us all uncertain and tentative about conveying our faith convictions.

In the midst of this world, Mount Seymour United Church made a decision to build a church and to nurture a Christian community. In the eyes of the world, this must seem a very foolish act. All that time, all that money, all that energy to keep the project going — surely, the world would think, there are better things to do.

At this point, our imaginations need to recall the tiny band of disciples, living in the midst of a decadent and power-hungry Roman empire. If they had waited for the approval of the world, wouldn't they still be waiting? Their journey to the cross becomes the paradigm of worldly foolishness. The only difference between them and us is that they encountered hostility; we more often experienced indifference.

Yet the story of that foolish journey is precisely what empowered a community like Mount Seymour United Church.

The decisions of the past ten years have been responsible, and yet, in the light of the sober statistical realities of our world, they were also moves of wild abandon. To continue the journey, this dynamic, of foolish risk for the sake of the transforming story we have to tell, must remain our constant companion.

The Reverend Brian Thorpe was minister to the Mount Seymour congregation from 1987 to 1994. His excellent communication skills were instrumental in guiding us through these very exciting and turbulent years. Brian is now General Secretary of B.C. Conference.

Even the best-laid plans can go awry. Siloam United, on the northern fringes of London, Ontario, could not have anticipated the serious illness of its minister, a driving force in its renewal, or a national recession, or a national controversy that hit the United Church hardest in its area.

8

A place
of healing

by Richard Hawley

Not far from Siloam United Church, there is a small country cemetery. It contains the graves of George Loveless, his wife, and his brothers.

Over the years, thousands of people have come from all over the world to visit these graves. George Loveless was a self-educated farmer in England, who began an agricultural union movement there. It was not popular among the landowners. In what is now recognized as a travesty of justice, Loveless and his friends were expelled in 1840 to what was then called Van Diemen's Land, now Tasmania, in Australia. A vigorous protest in England forced them to let Loveless return, but in 1844, he and his followers emigrated to Canada.

You may have heard of them, under a different name. They're most often recorded in history as the "Tolpuddle Martyrs."

They settled in the village of Fanshawe, near London, Ontario. There George Loveless became the founder and first lay preacher of the Siloam Circuit. He and his neighbours built the first log church.

No one knows for sure how the name Siloam came to be chosen for this community of faith, which was founded in 1857. Certainly, the reference is to the Pool of Siloam, fed by the waters of the Gihon

Spring through a tunnel built by King Hezekiah, deep under David's city, about 701 BCE. John's Gospel recalls a healing at that spring: "Go and wash in the pool of Siloam (which means 'sent forth'). Then he went and washed and came back able to see." (John 9:7)

Perhaps George Loveless sensed, in his vision of the stature and worth of all people, and in the dignity of the human spirit, a similar kind of healing based on the communion between God and humanity. Whatever the reasons, this is where a community of vision and healing began.

Urban expansion spills north

For many years, the congregation carried forward its vision and healing in a very rural community. The village of Fanshawe was out in the country, surrounded by fields of corn.

One of the saints of the church, from the 1930s to 1980, was Rose Burrell. Her home was directly across the road from the old church, which had no running water. Whenever the church held a supper or a special function, water was carried across the road in milk jugs.

Rose was always cheerful, always willing to work. She never complained or said anything unkind about anyone. She tended the shrubs and planted flowers around the church, carrying water from her home to help them grow.

Then in the 1970s the city of London began expanding its northern boundaries. The development of the Northridge subdivision brought Siloam new members. It was the beginning of a move away from Siloam's rural roots.

By 1984, the congregation circulated a survey to determine what direction the church should go, and what its future needs would be. A committee began investigating funding possibilities, and assessing the pros and cons of keeping the historic old building or building a brand new facility.

The consensus seemed to favour a new facility.

In 1985, the Church Development Committee was authorized to investigate acquiring land for a new building.

The guidance of a Mission Statement

At the same time, the congregation was developing a Mission Statement, to guide it through these new times.

Who are we?

We are a people who believe that our church is a place for spiritual renewal and growth and a place in which we learn about and engage in Christ's work of peace, love, and justice.

The church as the Body of Christ is a fellowship of hope, a family where we are welcomed, valued, needed and nurtured. As Christ's body, we are sent into the community and world to be witnesses.

What is our mission?

Our mission is to be a listening, learning, worshipping, teaching, caring community that addresses the spiritual, physical, intellectual and emotional needs of our church community and world family.

What shall we do?

1. Celebrate through the worship of God, the life of the church family.
2. Facilitate through Christian Education the growth in faith of all members of the church family.
3. Minister to the pastoral needs of our congregation, and the numerous identified United Church families and non-affiliated families in North London not attending a church.
4. Minister to the world through The United Church of Canada.

In order to do this more effectively, we believe that one of our most urgent needs is a building that will bring together our worshipping community and our church school; a facility that will be inviting and physically accessible to all.

In view of our understanding of the church, this facility should be one that will welcome and serve the congregation and the community, better enabling us to fulfil our mission to be Christ's presence in the world.

We must begin and continue to plan and build a facility using the resources and knowledge we have locally and those of the wider church.

Taking the plunge

A member of the congregation, Mabel Sproule, spurred the development by offering four acres of land, west of the old church, for one dollar. A year later, in 1986, the congregation applied for a Ventures in Mission loan of $300,000, approved the concept drawings for the new building, and let the contract for construction.

During 1988, the old building and the Christian Education Centre were sold. On June 26th, the Sunday morning worship service began in the old building and ended in the unfinished new sanctuary.

The new building's design attempted to capture the meaning of the Mission Statement. The building is totally accessible, at ground level, and all on one floor. The walls are glass, so that the inside can be seen invitingly from the outside; similarly, once you are inside, you cannot help but see outside, beyond the walls.

Troubled waters

The new building was dedicated on October 16, 1988. That year was, of course, one of great turmoil for The United Church of Canada, and the area around London was, perhaps, hardest hit with conflict. Some congregations split. Others lost large blocks of members. Siloam did not actually lose many members, but the congregation did not increase in size as had been forecast. Anticipated income did not come in, and therefore the debt, already large, grew.

The following year, the congregation was hit by further problems. The minister, Ken Martin, had been a driving force behind the new building. He suffered major health problems that forced him to resign on short notice. The congregation arranged first for a Sunday supply, and then for an interim ministry. Although the congregation sustained itself well through this period of crisis, once again anticipated growth did not — and perhaps could not — occur. By 1991, the debt had grown to over a million dollars.

My own ministry was established in April of 1991 and I immediately embarked on a continuing education program focused on New Church Development (NCD), for the whole congregation.

Neighbourhood gatherings brought together active and inactive families to share histories — their own, and the church's. The evenings always included some dreaming about the future. Eventually, these meetings moved to the financial concerns about the present.

The cottage meetings proved very successful in bringing inactive folk back to the church. They also initiated a movement to get a handle on the financial crisis. New financing was arranged with Ventures in Mission, and the congregation was able to reduce considerably its bank loan, then at 12% interest.

Mortgage meltdown

At that time, the congregation decided that its priority, for one year, needed to be the establishment of a sound financial base. A program called "Mortgage Meltdown" began. Committees and groups within the church all planned and executed a variety of fund-raising activities. Aside from the obvious goal of raising money, the primary goals of these activities were fun, creativity, and the involvement of as many people from the community as possible. The Stewardship and Finance Committee supported these efforts, while at the same time educating the congregation about stewardship.

The Committee also began building bridges to the United Church Council (related to NCD funding) and to the Presbytery as a whole. Both these efforts paid off when the Council provided a low interest loan to keep things afloat until the Mortgage Meltdown project was completed. The Council also gave a grant to the congregation, to increase the hours of the Staff Associate to three-quarter time.

If I had to pick out the single most positive force during the Meltdown campaign, it would have to be Mike Ashton, chair of the Stewardship and Finance Committee. Mike has a very positive outlook towards finances. He never talks about money. Instead, he describes the need to build resources to accomplish Siloam's mission. One Sunday he addressed the congregation and thanked everyone for their efforts: yard sale workers, pie makers, youth leaders, choir, volunteer cleaners, refugee committee... Never once did he mention money — he simply stressed the way we accomplish mission here.

It works! In two years, we managed to pay off $150,000 of our debt, while increasing staff and programs, and doing a lot of maintenance as well.

During this Mortgage Meltdown period, other significant things were happening too. The Staff Associate's increased hours allowed more programs and activities to develop. The music program was already strong; it grew still stronger. At the present time, Siloam has a senior choir of 45, a men's chorus, a women's chorus, a treble ensemble, youth singers, junior singers, and several instrumentalists — all of whom perform regularly.

New members bubble up

The Mortgage Meltdown program lasted from 1992 to 1993. During that time, the mortgage was reduced from $1,008,000 to $844,000.

By 1996 it was under $800,000. To give credit where it is due, much of this was achieved through the creative and positive leadership of the Stewardship and Finance Committee's treasurer, Bill Ashby, and the chair, Mike Ashton. In any NCD church, these two roles are essential. Today, although the congregation still has to struggle financially, its base is much more secure.

The congregation was still growing steadily — 590 in 1990, 631 in 1991, 678 in 1992, 734 in 1993. In 1996, 22 new members joined in January and another 51 in June. The majority of the new members have been 35 or younger. Thus the Sunday school program has also increased dramatically. Many of these new members are what is commonly called "unchurched." Some were once baptized and confirmed, and left the church entirely for a time. Others come with no church background at all.

Over and above the "full members," there are significant numbers of adherents still exploring their options. Several Roman Catholic spouses have chosen not to join the congregation, but are very active in its life.

These new folks indicate, when they are asked, that they come to the church for two reasons. They want a faith for themselves, and a place for their children to learn values for living in an increasingly complex world. Many have deep faith concerns. They have strong needs to develop relationships with others who are also searching for the same things. They say that they chose Siloam for the warmth they feel in this congregation, for the dynamic worship, for the meaningful Sunday school program they find for their children, and for a message that relates to the world in which they find themselves Monday to Saturday.

I think of some couples and individuals particularly.

Jim and Mary came to Siloam after attending a tableau of the Christmas story in one of the city parks. Their children had asked questions about the wise men and the shepherds, and they had no response. They knew the story, but realized that their children's only knowledge came through television. They decided to seek out a church where their children might learn more about the Bible. They now admit that they too have come to learn a great deal more about Jesus and his impact on the world.

Tom and Grace, an upper middle class couple, were similarly concerned that their children were getting all their values from television. Grace had been baptized Roman Catholic; Tom had no church experience. They chose a neighbourhood church, not for its denomination but its location. They have become active in the life of Siloam.

Edna and Bill grew up in the church. But after their children reached their teenage years, they quietly dropped away. Later, they began to feel a spiritual void in their lives. They did a lot of church shopping. They were looking for warmth of community, relevance of message, and a place where they felt they could belong. They're busy at Siloam now.

Ed is a single, middle-aged male. He came, I think, out of curiosity. Though he has no church background, he's interested in helping people. He has the resources to be generous, and he is.

Some have come to be married and stayed. Some have brought children for baptism and stayed. Keeping them requires work, by the minister and the congregation. We cannot simply expect them to return. They need encouragement.

The worship pool widens

By the fall of 1993, there had been enough growth that the congregation decided to start a second service. The sanctuary, which had once seemed much too big, was now too small to accommodate everyone. The single service had reached 80% capacity on average, and overflowed on special Sundays. The move to two services proved wise. The first Sunday it was done, the early service had 120 people attending, the second service 240. In total, that meant about 100 more people were worshipping than had worshipped on the previous Sundays.

Yet this was, after the decision to commence the building itself, one of the most difficult decisions that the congregation had to make. It meant that, almost inevitably, the sense of being a single large family would diminish, as the congregation evolved into two distinct and different groups of worshippers.

On occasions like Christmas Eve, the church had always been crowded. In anticipation, the congregation decided to hold three services. The total attendance that night was close to 1,000.

So far, the longer established members tend to alternate between services. New folks are more likely to choose one of the two Sunday services, and come to it on a regular basis.

Siloam now has three ministers. The Rev. John Lougheed was called for full time ministry with specific responsibilities in New Church Development. The Rev. Stan McDonald also ministers to the congregation on a part-time basis.

Siloam has not yet settled into a rut. Programs begin, end, and change as required. The music program continues to develop. Currently, much of the excitement centres on a growing interest in outreach. The congregation sponsors a Community Kitchen (where members gather once a month to cook communally and learn about menu planning and new recipes), a Food Cupboard (or food bank), Bosnian Medical Relief, and a refugee — as well as continuing to support The United Church of Canada's Mission and Service Fund.

It takes time and energy to get committees motivated and moving. This is especially true in New Church Development situations, where youth and lack of experience conspire to paralyse new beginnings. However, once started, youth and enthusiasm usually mean that committees work extremely well.

One and a half centuries or so after the congregation was founded by George Loveless, Siloam still sees itself as a place of healing, a place that is open to all, welcoming to all, where it is safe to build relationships and embark on a journey in faith. It has a vision of seeking to be witnesses to the community of the hope, love, forgiveness, and joy of Jesus Christ.

The Reverend Richard Hawley has been the minister of Siloam United since 1991. He is also president of the London Conference of the United Church of Canada.

Heritage United in Regina was just an offshoot of an existing congregation when it started. Being small taught it to discover and depend on its own people's skills and abilities, and to value the friendships that can grow in a close community.

$\mathcal{T}$he virtues
of starting small

by LOUISE GRAINGER

After a while, we got used to having a cougar looking down from his lofty perch at the people worshipping below. No one paid any attention to him. They just ignored him.

The cougar was the school mascot. After we had been worshipping in his school gym for quite a while, we took him for granted. But when we moved to our own facilities, we sort of missed him!

The launching of St. James the Second

Our encounter with the cougar started in 1979, when the northwest part of Regina was growing by leaps and bounds. New areas — Sherwood Estates, Walks Acres, McCarthy Park — were opening up. The closest United church was St. James' United. With this influx of new members, it was soon bulging at the seams. Something had to be done.

Soon, owing to the efforts of St. James' very competent ministers, the Rev. Tom Powell and the Rev. Rod Francis, it was announced that a new congregation had been formed, as a branch of St. James. It would be known as St. James the Second, with the St. James staff taking turns leading in worship.

In November 1979, services began in the St. Jerome School. Because we were a small congregation, people who probably were not aware of their gifts as leaders had to do their share. Soon we developed a foundational sense of community. Emphasis was on lay leadership. Because the staff team from St. James the First was very busy, this new congregation often had to make decisions on their own. Thus a great many leadership opportunities developed that probably would not have, in a larger and older congregation. As one member said, "We were the 18th family to join, and I was not here a month when I was asked to be on the council." Everyone had to be active.

With this steady growth eventually came our desire for independence. Five members of the congregation met, under the guidance of Tom Powell, to try to establish goals and to find the right direction in our quest for independence.

In 1980, in May, the Rev. Jeeva Sam joined us as a summer intern, bringing with him a special gift of music. That same year, Don McMillan was elected chair of Council, a position he held until his retirement in 1986. In 1981, another summer intern, Sheila Mallory, joined us and assisted in our first pamphlet drop to solicit new members through the neighbourhood.

In February 1982, the official boundaries of St. James the Second were set as "West of Pasqua St. and north of 9th Avenue North." Like Topsy from *Gone With the Wind*, our congregation just "growed and growed." Soon St. Jerome's School was too small. The new Centennial School was being built. After negotiating with the Board of Education, we moved there in September 1982. So it was that each Sunday, the cougar, a school emblem, looked down on us from his perch on the gym wall.

The birth of a new congregation

Everything was running smoothly, but we began to look to the future. We began to have new goals. We wanted to become an independent pastoral charge. In 1984, Regina Presbytery granted our request, and Heritage United Church was born.

In February, we began the task of calling our own minister. Because of our situation, the pattern of solid lay leadership had been long established, and we knew just how we wanted this leadership to work with the minister we would choose. As one member said, "The scripture reading that is important to us is the analogy of the body and

the church — we are all parts of the one body, and each part is important for the well-being of the whole."

The choice of our first minister was a good one. On April 8, a
congregational meeting was held. The following motion was made and
passed: "Moved and seconded that Presbytery ratify the calling of the
Rev. Ken Powers to be minister of Heritage United Church as of July
1st, 1984."

If starting small had been a benefit in encouraging people to apply
their gifts, Ken built on it. He was able to challenge people to use gifts
before they knew they had them — to support them, and then to leave
them to stand on their own. Ken does not preach to us, as one congregation member said; "He talks, he tells stories, he explains the Bible,
he gets his point across. I feel he is speaking to me, not preaching at
me. We don't always agree, but that is okay."

Ken loves to sing. He and our music director, Diane Taylor, a highly
talented choir leader who joined us in 1986, did many special things
for people through their music. If you weren't a singer before you
came to our church, you soon ended up being one. With Ken's beautiful voice leading us, we learned to appreciate music more than ever.

You might think that with all this, we would sit back and relax.
But no, the momentum of growth continued. We began to look for
adequate office space for our new minister. We found it in the fall of
1984.

Now that we had offices, we hired Val Gudmundson as our secretary that December. The office was also used for meetings, Bible study
groups, choir practice, and other events. But soon this space became
too small; more adequate space was needed.

In 1985, we became proud owners of 1.85 acres of land. Funds
were now made available from Regina Presbytery, for building. Our
congregation purchased and moved a mobile home to our new acreage. Perhaps, to others in the community, this lonely mobile home
sitting there amongst the weeds didn't look like much. But to us it was
a thing of beauty, mice and all. We began to dream that maybe, someday, we would erect our own church here.

In May, Helen Anderson was hired to replace Val, who retired as
secretary.

Focusing our vision

The idea for a mission statement developed in October 1986. In
an article in *The United Church Observer*, regional editor Deana Driver
reported that the need for a mission statement was first kindled at a

New Church Development workshop. The workshop was told that having a mission statement helps you know who you are and where you are going. At a November worship service, three members of an ad hoc committee — Marj Kent, Denis Walters (chair of the long range planning committee) and Leanne Eldridge (a young member of the outreach committee) talked about the weekend workshop and the need for a mission statement. They also presented a puppet show that outlined the history of the congregation.

Thus was the stage set for preparing a mission statement.

Some of our members had been involved in developing *The Whole People of God* Sunday school curriculum. We'd had representatives on Conference and National church committees. And our lay people had many times led our Sunday services. So the committee working on a mission statement felt that the word "faith" should be included. Another word they considered relevant was "caring," since we not only sponsored a refugee family from Eritrea but also supported the food bank, Regina's downtown chaplaincy, and other services. Two more phrases that appealed to the committee were "caring for the people of God" and "witnessing through action."

A good deal of discussion, drafting, and rewriting ensued. Finally the committee came up with a recommended mission statement. At the October 1987 Council meeting of Heritage United Church, the following statement was adopted:

> *Our challenge is to be*
> *a caring people of God:*
> *growing in faith,*
> *developing friendships,*
> *witnessing through action,*
> *and nurturing our hopes*
> *for the future.*

This mission statement sounded great, but were we really capable of putting it into action?

We were soon put to the test. A month after Lorne Crawford and his wife June joined our church in 1984, he had a second heart attack. They were a cheery couple who took an active part in our church. Lorne always had a smile to greet you with. Lorne was diagnosed as a prime candidate for a heart transplant, and so they journeyed to London, Ontario, in the hope that he would not have long to wait for a donor. It was a time of stress, anxiety, and often despair for them as they waited and waited.

Their church family did indeed live up to its mission statement. It rallied to their support with prayers, phone calls, letters, cards, a monetary gift to help with expenses, and many other offers to help, to get them through this critical time. June said later that knowing their church family was there for support helped them get through many dark moments. Ken Powers was able to visit them, and to add his personal support, and to help heighten their hopes that all would be fine.

Finally, in 1988 — after four years of uncertainty — a donor was found, and Lorne received his new heart. Our own hearts filled with joy, and we gave many thankful prayers to God for giving Lorne a new life.

At this time we discovered just how talented our music director and our minister really were. They composed the first of many new songs for us. That first song was titled "A New Heart," and it was dedicated to Lorne:

> *A new heart I will give you,*
> *A new hope for today,*
> *A new heart and a new hope*
> *And strength to walk the way.*

On the move again

By this time, we were quite settled in with the gym as our place of worship. Yes, it was a lot of work putting out the chairs and taking them down each Sunday, moving the piano out and putting our banners up, but everyone pitched in.

Then, slowly but steadily, a gentle protest was heard from the Sunday school, like the murmur of waves of a calm sea caressing the shore. We had a large Sunday school, and children were crammed into every available space for their lessons. There were just too many of them for the cold locker rooms, the drafty foyer, and the halls. And from the looks of many of the mothers, our attendance was soon going to rise even higher.

We also needed space for our mid-week groups and programs.

Thus we were pushed to taking still another step on our journey, but this time it was to be more than just a step. It would have to be a giant leap. We were talking about building our own church. Could those dreams finally become a reality?

The decision to build our own church was not an easy one, and certainly not one to be taken lightly. It would entail a lot of planning, work, and funding. It was a time of doubt, apprehension, and tension. And of a lot of "what ifs." What if we can't raise the money? What if our projected future congregation doesn't materialize? What if we become so big we lose our identity?

Becoming too large was a genuine concern for us, for starting small had given us the opportunity, as one lay person said, "to build a foundational sense of community." Another added, "People were given the opportunity to find their own gifts. Those who became part of the congregation had ability, but many who are now seen as gifted might not have discovered those gifts without the encouragement they received."

We did not want to lose those people, or their gifts.

Time progressed. The congregation was asked for their input and opinions. Planning was done. Many options were discussed. Finally, we decided that we would go ahead.

The decision was not unanimous. A few families opted out. They felt we were going too fast. We hated to see them leave, but that was their decision.

A building committee was appointed, with Denise Walters as chair. A very active, dedicated, committee, they put in long hours of hard work. At a series of dessert parties, hosted by the Long Range Planning Committee, the congregation was asked for input. The congregation overwhelmingly asked for open space, lots of windows, lots of light, and plenty of classrooms that could be made larger or smaller.

Acting on these priorities, and using the role of the church as defined in the mission statement, the committee came up with a draft plan. The architectural firm of Argot, Kelley and Associates was chosen, and the committee worked closely with Ben Kelley to work out the details. Ben found the mission statement most helpful in drawing up the plans. Though it was back to the drawing board many times, he soon had a scale model made so that everyone could see and discuss the proposal.

The mission statement was also helpful to the congregation, for it helped in securing Ventures in Mission funding for us. Throughout

1987 and 1988, our proposal had been presented, with the necessary documents, to Presbytery, Conference, and finally to National committees. The mission statement helped to answer many of their questions about why we were doing certain things and we received good support at every level. As one congregation member said, "We gave them a careful response to each request for information."

When the final plans were approved by Presbytery, the chair of its Property Committee told us they were approved without needing any discussion at all because "you had done your work so well at every stage. You knew what you were doing, and we trusted you. You have been put through the wringer on several occasions, and we knew you were ready."

Farewell to the cougar

On Sunday October 9, 1988, we had a sod-turning ceremony. It started with our regular service at Centennial school, after which our congregation proudly marched to the site, carrying a banner that said "Shalom." The Rev. Gail Christi, chair of Presbytery, assisted by five-year-old Jeremy Walters, turned the first ceremonial sod.

Over a bitter Saskatchewan winter, the building took shape. The waiting was hard. We wanted the workers to hurry, hurry, hurry. Eagerly we watched each part of the construction. But the congregation was not left out of the work. As the rooms took shape, many came wielding their paint brushes and helping in other ways. After all, this was our church, and we were going to have a hand in its construction. Besides, it was a fun time for us.

By March 6, 1989, the building was complete enough for the first Council meeting to be held there. It was a good meeting — despite the fact that there wasn't any furniture yet, and the walls were still bare and unpainted. The members of the Council sat on folding chairs that they had brought themselves.

The church was nearing completion, and so we formed a Celebration committee to come up with ideas how best to celebrate the happy occasion when our church was finally ready for us. Galena Gudmunson, one of our young members, volunteered to be on this committee. She was warmly welcomed — and in the end, it was her idea that we used.

May 7, 1989, was the great day. After our last service at Centennial school, we gathered up all our worship paraphernalia: hymn books, banners, cloths for the table, etc. We passed out bright colourful bal-

loons. The children especially liked this idea — though a few escaped
from little hands and floated up to the ceiling of the gym, a bright
reminder that we had been there. Leaving the cougar to watch these
errant balloons, we processed out into a bright but chilly May day.
Ken and Diane had written a new song especially for this occasion. A
straggly but happy group sang words that described our history as a
congregation with joy in our voices:

We're on the move
Praise God, we're on the move!
We're on the move,
Praise God, we're on the move!
We're on the move
We're on the move
We are God's people on the move!

We proudly marched the few blocks to our new home.

And there it was, welcoming us into its brightly lit foyer. We quickly
toured our house of faith. Though the chairs had not yet been set up
and the centrum lacked wallpaper, we couldn't help getting lumps in
our throats, we couldn't help feeling a sense of accomplishment and
pride, as we gathered in the centrum for prayer and song. The children loved their new Sunday school area. The coloured balloons drifted
upwards to a new ceiling over us.

Our journey of faith had led us to this warm and welcoming place
— our church.

And so we moved in. A bright brass plaque bearing our mission
statement greets you as you enter the large, bright, foyer. Soft shades
of grey and rose wallpaper in the centrum, and the many windows,
make you welcome. Through the windows that circle the choir loft
and the pulpit, you can look out and see the soft falling snow, an airplane
climbing upward, the geese v-ing for their long journey south.

Maintaining that family feeling

We settled nicely into our new house of worship. The transition
went smoothly, probably because we carried with us the original sense
of family and belonging together. As one member stated, "We value
the building, but we don't make a big fuss about it. The building didn't

come out of wanting a grand place to worship, it came out of a need to serve the people during mid-week, and we needed the building for Sunday school. If it was just a place for worship that we needed, we could have survived in the gym."

Another said, "I don't ever hear people defining themselves in terms of the building. We are a church congregation. We are a community. If we were without the building, we could still be the same congregation, same community."

Our first proper service was held in our new church on Pentecost Sunday, May 14th, 1989. On Sunday, September 10, an evening dedication service was held with the Rev. Jeeva Sam representing Presbytery. He presented the keys to the building to Denise Walters, chair of the Building Committee, who accepted them on behalf of the congregation. Rod Dumontel accepted a picture as a gift from the architects. A newspaper report stated, "For the first time in 10 years, The United Church of Canada dedicated a new church building in Regina."

We had chosen to sit on chairs instead of pews, because we wanted this large room to be used for other functions, not just for church services. The chairs can be quickly taken out, and then the whole room utilized. It is used for brunches, fowl suppers, fashion shows, clothing sales... Other groups in the community, such as Tai Kwan Do, Jazzercise, a private nursery school, Brownies, etc., rent it. This not only helps others, but generates much needed revenue. One of the children saw a TV show that portrayed a church with pews, and commented, "I like our chairs better."

We have striven to be an inclusive church, a family church, welcoming all ages, all people who have wanted to be a part of our nucleus. Like any family, we have had good times and bad. There have been times of great stress, times of anger, and even hostility, and times of sadness and hurt. Many of these emotions came into play during the debate, in the national church, over the issue of ordaining homosexual candidates. A few people left. We were sorry to lose them. But the rest of us rallied around, and I believe we are stronger for having gone through this trying time together. Like any family, you do not run from conflict — you stick together and work it through.

When Lorne Crawford died, we wept for his family, but we also wept for ourselves, for we had all lost a friend. Our floor has been a problem; our debt load is horrendous, a matter of great concern and worry. We overworked some of our volunteers, and a few have felt burnt out. But despite these crises and heartaches, we still feel we are one family, one of togetherness.

We have had many happy times too. Laughter is no stranger to our church. Making hearts for Valentines is always fun. All ages take part, male and female — eating the bits of chocolate left over is the best part. The Adult Social Club has good times, as does the Catering Group when they plan and prepare for special events. The choir too gives us many moments of pleasure. In December 1989, the choir presented a musical story called "Joseph and Mary: A Love Story." This play, like many of our hymns, was composed by Ken and Diane, and became a Christmas special on TV on the CanWest network and on Spirit Connection, the United Church program on Vision TV.

I would be remiss not to mention our children, including the Youth Choir, for they give us many hours of pleasure and happiness. They are an important part, if not the most important part, of our church family. They delight us with their recitations and plays from Sunday school, and they take an active part in our baptism ceremonies and in communion.

Togetherness is a key word. People sense this as they worship with us. There is a real feeling of friendship here. Recently I was at a dinner that included four different families. These people had all become friends through our church. As the evening progressed, I could see that the church was not just a Sunday experience, but was a part of their daily lives. As one person said, "We care for one another, not just as fellow members of the United Church but also as friends. We have found that we can disagree on things and still remain friends."

Not standing still

Now we must continue to move, in a new direction. We must stand back and view our aims, to see whether or not our mission statement is still relevant today — or does it need restructuring. We are growing in numbers — so much so that we now must hold a second service on Saturday. As we mature as a congregation, we must take another look at the role we want our minister to play, remembering that he cannot be all things to all people.

We have reached our physical goal on our journey of faith, but we must continue on our spiritual journey. We know that as we travel this road, there will be many detours and bumps. But if we continue to challenge ourselves, continue to develop friendships, continue to keep our church an inclusive church, we will also continue to be caring people of God, growing in faith.

Louise Grainger is 68 years old and has two daughters and three grandsons: a 13 year old and 2-year-old twins. She began writing at age 50 and has published short stories. At Ogema United Church she was secretary to the minister, served on the personnel committee and council, and taught Sunday school for 14 years. She became a member of Heritage United in 1983 when she moved to Regina. She now writes for the newsletter and does other behind the scenes work, preferring to let the younger people take the more active roles.

In many ways, Edmonton's Kirk United Church could be considered typical of the congregations founded during the boom years of the 1950s and '60s, moving now into its middle-age. and making adjustments along the way. After a virile youth and early adulthood, it was joined in partnership, first by Westminster United, and then a few years later by Central United, and began the next phase of its journey.

10

$\mathcal{N}$ostalgia and hope

by COPIE MACMILLAN

In Scotland and in the Presbyterian tradition, a church is often called a "kirk." On that basis, the name "Kirk United Church" sounds redundant.

But in fact, it was named for a minister who was never really our minister, and his wife who ministered to us without being a minister.

To unravel all those complexities, you have to go back to the early 1950s. World War II had recently ended. Edmonton was booming with oil, construction, and service industries. And babies. A thousand people a month were flooding into Edmonton, swelling the suburbs daily. New communities of Sherbrooke, Dovercourt, and Woodcroft were opening up to supply housing. A new school opened every year: Sherbrooke in 1954, Woodcroft in 1955, Dovercourt in 1956.

In those days, where there were people, there must be a church. In 1953, Sunday school classes for Kindergarten to Grade 9, were started by a Women's Auxiliary circle from McDougall United Church as an extension project. Classes were held in the basements of homes within the community. In 1954 the Sunday school moved to the new Sherbrooke School, under the direction of Mrs. W. Morgan, a diaconal minister from the Extension Department of Edmonton Presbytery.

In 1955, Edmonton Presbytery asked Mrs. Clara Kirk to take over the extension work in this booming new area. Her husband, the Rev. Joe E. Kirk, on leave because of ill health, encouraged her to take on this task. He himself took the Sunday services until his death December 30 that same year. Undaunted, Mrs. Kirk continued with the extension work. The Rev. J. R. Geeson, a retired minister, provided worship leadership. He also helped with a door-to-door visitation, which brought about a meeting of a group of interested people, April 18, 1956, to apply to Presbytery to be recognized as a congregation. They wanted to found a church in the community.

Since a church requires a name, the congregation-to-be voted to name the church "Kirk" United Church, in recognition of the work of The Reverend and Mrs. J. E. Kirk.

Every year, a new record

Then began a period of spectacular growth. At the service of constitution June 10, 1956, 227 people joined as charter members. There was no church building yet, of course, so meetings were held in homes, and people gave unstintingly of their time. Then, as now, a lunch was served at every meeting. Boards and committees were formed. Richard Martin, in his final year of theology at St. Stephen's College, was appointed as Student Supply to Kirk until his ordination the following May.

By Easter Sunday 1957, there were over 500 people at two services.

There were so many children, the Sunday school had to run two shifts, one at 9:45, the other at 11:00 a.m. Enrolment began at 300; by the end of the year, it had risen to 400.

The Women's Auxiliary, later to become the United Church Women, grew from one Unit to seven under Mrs. Kirk's continued leadership. A choir was organized, a piano purchased. Mid-week groups quickly followed: Explorers, Cubs, CGIT, and a Couples' Club.

With Howard Lucas as its editor, the monthly edition of *The Friendly Kirk* was published. This newspaper was published for several years, with Bob Stark succeeding Howard Lucas as its editor. Those issues are a gold mine of information about those early years.

To call a minister, the congregation needed to have a manse available. With the energy and commitment typical of those boom years, they built one in 11 weeks. The Rev. Ian Macmillan was called to serve as Kirk's minister on August 1, 1957. On September 20, Mr. Macmillan and his family moved into the manse. The first Bible study class was held in their basement.

A new building in less than a year

Then came the building programs. There were some significant dates:

- May 4, 1958: Sod turning ceremony for the Christian Education Building.
- December 1958: 100 young people formed the "Teen Church" using space in the Seventh Day Adventist School across the street.
- March 29, 1959: The C.E. Building was completed. Church services, mid-week groups, and Sunday school invaded every square inch. The first church service was held there on Easter Sunday.
- May 23, 1959: The first wedding at Kirk. Appropriately, it was the wedding of Pat Wheeler and Dr. Donald Kirk, the son of the Reverend and Mrs. Kirk.

Eventually Reverend Macmillan was called to another church. The Rev. Blair McPherson accepted a call from Kirk in June 1961. Sunday school enrolment that year soared to over **800**, with an average attendance around 525. Enrolment in mid-week groups was also high.

In 1962, the Women's Auxiliary became the UCW; the Men's Club held a $10 a plate dinner to pay off the organ. In June 1964, thanks to the UCW, the mortgage on the manse was burned.

In September 1964, the congregation voted to proceed with building a sanctuary. Things moved fast. The cornerstone was laid October 10. A year later, in December 1965, the Christmas morning service was held in the new sanctuary; on January 2, 1966, the dedication service was held.

Changing times and demographics

The Rev. Douglas Weatherburn accepted Kirk's call in 1967. The congregation revised its structure to create a Unified Board from the former Session and Stewards in 1969. In 1971, under Weatherburn's guidance, outreach services began in the neighbouring Norwood-McGugan Extended Care Institute. Thanks to some very dedicated people, these monthly services are still going strong.

The next minister to accept a call to Kirk, in 1974, was the Rev. Ray Leppard. The following year, he attended the Bethel Bible Study

Training Course in Madison, Wisconsin. The Bethel program, a comprehensive overview of the Bible, comprised of four seven-week semesters over two years, is demanding, but fulfilling. Under Ray Leppard's guidance, ten teachers were recruited from the congregation to take the two-year training course. The classes they eventually led proved very successful, with over 100 people attending. The Bethel programs continued at Kirk for over 16 years, with a second and then a third group of trained teachers.

In June 1981, Kirk celebrated its 25th Anniversary. The story of Kirk was printed, giving a brief summary of the church's growth and history. The anniversary party lasted the whole weekend, starting with a concert on the Friday evening, continuing with a banquet Saturday, and ending with worship on Sunday. Former members came from as far away as Toronto, Peachland in B.C., and Calgary. That Sunday, 30 new members joined.

Although boom years never last forever, Kirk has been fortunate to have continued growth and success. Much of the credit has been due to Ray Leppard, his wife Enid, and his family, working in harmony with many other dedicated and caring people. In August 1994, the congregation celebrated 20 years of Ray Leppard's ministry at Kirk. Kirk's experience suggests that long-term ministries can be a definite asset to a congregation.

Amalgamation brings new talents

In the meantime, of course, the world has been changing all around Kirk. While Kirk has prospered, other congregations have not. People no longer consider a church to be a necessary part of a community. Once-thriving churches find their budgets and their memberships declining, until the only reasonable solution becomes amalgamation with another like-spirited congregation.

In the last half-dozen years, Kirk United has benefited from two of these amalgamations.

On April 21, 1991, Westminster United joined with Kirk to become one congregation. There was a short service at Westminster, attended by a number of Kirk members. Then the Kirk members escorted the Westminster congregation to Kirk and welcomed them to their new home.

The on November 27, 1994, families from Central United were embraced by Kirk with a special Welcoming Service, and amalgamation took place with their congregation.

Both congregations brought with them their stories, their expertise and years of service, their banners, their symbols and memorials, their artefacts. In Kirk's sanctuary, we became one. The Westminster and Central people brought with them many talents and much experience, and a friendliness that adds greatly to the whole congregation.

Since 1989, Kirk has had two "plus" ministers. The Rev. Sydney Bell first joined Kirk as part-time staff in 1989. He is now retired, but is Kirk's minister emeritus. Syd served Central United for several years in the '80s, and had an important role to play as Central folk struggled to decide on their future church home. He continues to be actively involved at Kirk.

The Rev. Neil Lemke accepted a call to join Dr. Leppard in team ministry at Kirk in July 1992, and added a new dimension to the life of the congregation. He was no stranger to the congregation, though, for he had been a student intern with us a few years before.

In fact, Kirk United has a proud record as a "teaching church" — for since the beginning of the congregation, no fewer than 15 student interns, from theological colleges all across Canada, have trained at Kirk.

Upon his retirement, in June 1995, the congregation bid a fond farewell to the Rev. Dr. Ray and to Mrs. Enid Leppard, and honoured, in a variety of ways, their 21 years of ministry at Kirk.

Rev. J. Paul Mullen and his wife Jeanne accepted Kirk's call in July 1995, to join in team ministry with the Rev. Neil Lemke and his wife Carrie.

Of historical note is the fact that on July 27, 1995, Mrs. Clara **Kirk** was honoured on her 95th birthday. She no longer is able to attend church services, but has, until fairly recently continued to worship at Kirk United and attend its congregational functions.

So there have been many opportunities — and a real necessity — for Kirk's ministry and mission to grow. We are no longer a young church — more middle-aged and maturing. With the three congregations combined, we have once again a rich mix of ages and stages. There are many seniors now, and quite a few *senior* seniors. But also, once more, there are young families, and we see toddlers and little ones all over the place again. For those who remember the early years, it's a delightful feeling of *déjà vu*.

Where once the congregation needed all of the available facilities for its own purposes, several non-profit community groups now use the building for their meetings. In addition, committees within the church are planning more outreach programs. One example, is the Community Kitchen Project, organized through the Church in Society Committee. This is a program for families of low income, to train participants in the preparation of low-cost nutritious meals. The group meets twice a month — once to plan and once to cook. Participants pay a minimal amount, and take home the food that has been prepared.

Community outreach has become a prominent element of Kirk's ministry. Weddings, baptisms, funerals, counselling, bible study, and visiting are all high priorities. Kirk's Pastoral Care Volunteer Network, consisting of about 25 to 30 men and women, makes over 100 calls a month to hospitals, nursing homes, seniors, shut-ins, and those ill at home. It also provides a grief ministry. Friends from Norwood-McGugan Extended Care are brought to Kirk once a month to join in worship and the friendship/refreshment hour that follows, in addition to our ongoing monthly worship services at their facilities. Kirk is also actively involved in supporting, in a variety of ways, the programs and needs of Bissell Centre, serving Edmonton's inner city.

World outreach could be improved, although support for Mission and Service is fairly generous.

Still building

In the summer of 1993, with some of the funds resulting from the sale of Westminster Church, the narthex of Kirk was extended to become a chapel. The Rev. Sydney Bell, minister emeritus, conducted the first wedding in the chapel February 24, 1994.

There is an upbeat and happy feeling in our church as we work to assimilate the changes in our congregation and staff over the past few years, and to plan ways to deal with the challenges of the present and the future.

So we look back with nostalgia, and look forward with hope.

Copie MacMillan and her husband Jack have been active members of Kirk since its constitution in 1956. Copie has served the local congregation and the greater arenas of the church in a variety of capacities, including Clerk of Session, Chair of the Worship and Congregation Committees, Roll Clerk, Presbytery Rep, conference delegate, Intern Support Committee member, CGIT leader, Sunday school and Bethel Bible school teacher, etc. etc. "Simply **busy** *in the life and work of the church" during her 40 year relationship with Kirk, she says.*

Building and maintaining networks, both inside and outside the congregation, was an essential component of Orléans United Church's growth in a new suburban community outside of Ottawa.

11

Children in the forefront

by LINDA ACTON-RIDDLE

The children's stories told by our first minister, Joanne Barr, were the highlight of the service each Sunday morning. She was a magnet to the children in the congregation.

One Sunday she brought them to the front to learn a prayer. At the end of the prayer, one little girl crossed herself as Roman Catholics do. Joanne looked up at the congregation. "I can see," she said "the results of kindergarten in the Separate School System."

The city of Orléans, Ontario, was growing so quickly, bringing in so many new families with young children, that the local schools could not keep up with the demand. The public schools particularly could not provide enough spaces for four-year-old junior kindergarten classes. The result was that many parents, including our minister, sent their four-year-olds to the Roman Catholic schools where there was still space, planning to switch them back to the public schools afterwards.

From convent to new community

It was only fitting. Not many years before, Orléans had been a tiny Franco-Ontarian village. Then some land belonging to one of the religious orders was sold. In the 1970's, the developers found a ready market in young families — grown-up baby boomers with their new families — looking for housing near Ottawa. Many were members of the Canadian Armed Forces, the RCMP, Bell Telephone, or the Civil Service; most of them worked in Ottawa only 15 minutes away.

During 1978, a group of people sat together on the bus commuting into work each morning. In their conversations the need for a local United Church came up. One of those people, the Rev. Dave Estey, was a chaplain in the Canadian Forces. Through his contacts in Presbytery, the initial steps were taken: Ottawa Presbytery was approached about starting a congregation and it offered both verbal and financial support.

There was a joint Anglican/United Church congregation already meeting in an elementary school each Sunday, but the need for a separate, United Church was apparent. This was to be the first wholly United Church congregation in Orléans. Presbytery approved an experimental program and appointed a minister. The word quickly spread to people wishing to return to church, and to people who had been travelling into Ottawa to attend United Churches there. The pianist came from the local United/Anglican congregation; so did the printing of our first bulletin. Hymn books were loaned from another Anglican parish.

Temporary stopping places

In the beginning, we met in the gymnasium of Cairine Wilson Secondary School. The first service was held at 8:30 a.m. on January 7, 1979. Our funding was a block grant from Presbytery for a trial period of 3 months, later extended to 6 months. Soon after that, the experimental project was elevated to "mission field" status. Because of the network of contacts that some people (especially Dave Estey) had with older established churches and with the Canadian Forces chapels, we were loaned or given the basic furniture for worship, including service books, communion trays and collection plates. Bible study groups were formed by interested people to fulfil the need for spiritual growth during the week.

Within 13 months we outgrew that first location and moved to Garneau High School. This one had an amphitheatre that was ideal for a sanctuary; the numerous classrooms were quickly filled with all ages of young children. Another advantage was that not one of our Sunday school children attended this French-language school during the week. Our meeting time Sunday morning changed from 8:30 to 10:00, the storage was a little better, and since we didn't have to scurry out of the way of another congregation coming in, we could visit over coffee afterwards.

The coffee hour was important in our growth. The church community was building and the strength we were developing in our friendships was important to our growth in numbers. We discovered coworkers, neighbours, and former acquaintances at church. At the same time, we developed new friendships and introduced neighbours, coworkers, and friends to others in our congregation.

A membership without church roots

Most of us had drifted away from attending regular church services after we left our home churches as teens or young adults. Many were now looking for a warm church experience in which to bring up our children. This network of young families with similar dreams and aspirations was a binding force on which our congregation was building in numbers. There were few people of retirement age in Orléans; it was a community of middle-aged people and younger parents.

The parents' backgrounds were varied. Many of us were from non-United Church backgrounds. A large number were of Roman Catholic backgrounds. This brought a richness of experience to the congregation and a wider understanding that had not been as evident in our own growing up years.

But because of their unfamiliarity with United Church customs, we had to do a lot of educating about our policies and organization.

Joanne Barr, the first minister appointed by Presbytery, was great at allowing people to complete the task she had asked them to do without interfering. Her confidence developed a sense of pride in our own abilities and a trust with the minister and later other staff people. Since her position as minister was only part-time and the tasks of ministry had to be rounded out by the members of the congregation, our lay involvement started right from the beginning.

The vibrancy of the services was infectious. We sang new hymns that seemed more relevant to us, tried out different music, and were even filmed on the CBC television program *Meeting Place*. Church was exciting, and called us to be involved.

In March 1981 we voted to change the name of our church from Convent Glen to Orléans United, to indicate that it was for the whole city, and not just for one neighbourhood. The decision recognized that we would be continually growing as the city expanded; we would attempt to serve the whole area and would probably become a large congregation.

It was an exciting time for our small group of parishioners. We felt like a family on the verge of a new stage of development.

By the middle of 1983 our first minister, Joanne Barr, had left for another position. We had the difficult task of choosing our own minister for the first time. Most of us had never been through this process before, either as leaders or as committee members. We had been older adolescents or very young adults — if we had been around in our home churches at all — when this procedure had last taken place. However, under guidance from people at Presbytery, we formed a committee and made our first selection.

It was an adjustment for the children especially; this next minister was a male, the Rev. Jamie Gosse. They had grown used to a mother figure. Now they had to relate to a father figure.

Needing a permanent church home

The process of transforming the school cafetorium into a worship sanctuary each Sunday morning was a massive undertaking. Lunch tables needed to be moved out. Chairs, lectern, communion table, piano, and hymn books had to be moved in. Each Sunday morning a team moved into the school one and a half hours before the service to work at this job. Some dashed home after helping to set up in order to take a shower and get dressed before returning for the service.

This "before service" and "after service" labour began to take its toll. We started to look at the possibility of having our own church building as a simpler method of worshipping. Our church committees were growing in size and number and had no regular place to meet. Our homes had to take on the slack of storage and meeting requirements. It was a great way to get to know one another, but we still lacked a common meeting place during the week.

Our new minister helped us take the next step in our growth — choosing a parcel of land on which to build eventually. We chose a corner lot, back near our first location, and Presbytery purchased it. In September 1983 we held a "Service of Land Dedication" on the site. Now we could look at the location as we drove past and try to imagine our church building on it. We delivered information flyers in the area a few times. On the urging of Dave Patterson, a founding member and quiet leader in the congregation, I painted a large sign advertising the site as the future home of Orléans United Church and a group dug post holes and erected it. People spoke about it to one another as they passed it on the street and we overheard them in the stores as well as at social functions. The town was becoming a city. Word was spreading. And our congregation continued to grow!

As the new year, 1984, dawned, we commissioned a Planning Committee to conduct a Building Feasibility Study. Yes, we were interested in having our own structure, but could we afford to take on such a venture?

Despite tragedy, growth continues

Tragedy struck us in February when Jamie Gosse died suddenly. We were shaken. Our leader was no longer there to lead; our young family was fatherless. We wondered if we could continue as a congregation. Within days ordinary people with strong faith and valuable skills stepped into the role of counsellors, leaders, preachers, and advisors. We soon realized that this family of Orléans United was a strong bond. The many roles a minister plays were taken on by very capable people from our midst. We had always had a strong and wide lay involvement and it became even more apparent during this difficult period. Under the direction of the Worship Committee a number of lay people had planned and conducted Sunday services during the summer months when the minister was on holiday. Now the same people and more stepped in to help and offer their talents. It was a time both of mourning and of self discovery. It was the first death that most of the children had experienced first hand.

Again the networks we had developed within the United Church community came to our aid. Dave Patterson had been taking a course from the Rev. Tom Sherwood, a friend of Jamie's. Tom was teaching at Carleton University and St. Paul University and was available the following Sunday to lead us in a worship service of grief, acceptance, and renewal. He counselled the children to help them understand and to put the death into some perspective.

When he returned for a second Sunday, a month later, we began to talk among ourselves about our feeling that he was the minister with whom we wanted to work. We were very pleased when he accepted our formal call in June 1984.

At the Annual General Meeting in January 1985, the congregation voted to build a house of worship. Each step along the way was decided by the Planning Committee, one of the many other committees, or a vote by the full congregation. Loans were approved, an architectural firm was hired, a design was chosen. We all suggested changes in design, we proposed technical improvements such as a sound booth from which to control microphones and record the services, we voted on colours, exterior and interior finish, and we began fund-raising events with a flourish. We felt it was definitely going to be our House of Worship.

I remember the sod-turning day on Palm Sunday afternoon of 1988. The grounds were rather low lying and water lay on the ground. Being March, the earth was still frozen solid. Cameras recorded this historic slice of time as local dignitaries spoke of the excitement this project was generating in the community. Everyone felt a special twinge of pride. It was one of the first new church buildings within the mushrooming city. Our shovels couldn't penetrate into the ice and frozen ground but we managed a few little ceremonial scoops to mark the occasion.

A crucial decision about direction

Our congregation had made the monumental decision to build a church building. We already had a church. Now we needed a building to house our worship, to meet in during the week, to be more of a physical presence in the community, and to be a place of outreach.

The size and shape of the structure had been decided. A Ventures in Mission (VIM) loan had been granted to us, additional smaller loans were made available by Presbytery, and the bank had arranged a loan to cover the rest of the mortgage.

But now we faced another decision. Should we try to squeeze all of us into one service? Or should we go to two services each Sunday, to make room for newcomers we hadn't yet met? As Superintendent of the already large Sunday school, I spoke up and stated that I thought it was crucial that we change to two full services each Sunday morning. We already were using 19 classrooms in the high school for Sunday school each Sunday morning. How could we possibly accommodate that number in our own church building in just one service? We were already combining a few age groups in the classrooms in order to accommodate all of the students. The classrooms in the high school were larger than our study rooms would be in our own structure.

What a wonderful dilemma! We had too many children for just one service in a church building we hadn't even moved into yet!

But make no mistake — it *was* a dilemma. We had built a wonderful network of dedicated people working together. We all knew one another, recognized one another's children, ministered to one another during the coffee hour afterwards. If we had two regular services we feared we would not stay the cohesive group we had become during that large single service. It was frightening to think that we might not be able to worship all together at the same time, visit with each other every week, check up on others' stresses at work and at home, give and take advice from other members we trusted and who had become our friends. Some felt it would split us into two separate congregations in the same church. It wouldn't be like a small family anymore; it would be more like distant cousins passing each other as one left the first service and the other arrived for the second service. Would two services destroy what we had worked so hard to become? Or would it just change us, challenge us to keep important contacts, allow more room for newcomers, give space for spiritual and physical growth?

We discussed this dilemma at church during the service, during coffee hour afterwards, at home over the phone, in the local stores, and at work. Tom Sherwood led us in thoughtful discussion. Finally the decision was made. We began the two service, two Sunday school, format in September 1988 for the last four months in the high school. This would prepare us for our move into our own building at Christmas time.

We have continued that format ever since with full services and Sunday school at 9 a.m. and 11 a.m., except during July and August when we move down to one service. For several years now we have also added a year-round alternative to Sunday morning: a Saturday evening service from Labour Day to Victoria Day and a Thursday evening service through the summer. Each Sunday morning we now have two identical services in the sanctuary at 9 and 11 a.m. with 8 to 10 Sunday school classes during each of the services. We needed to keep in contact with one another. The coffee hour between the services would be the first chance in the week to keep in touch. Other chances would come throughout the week at committee meetings and church social events.

Born on Christmas Eve

During the spring and summer of 1988 the construction site was a hive of activity. Members of the congregation were not allowed to assist at the very beginning but as soon as the foundation was laid the teams of workers descended. After the steel beams were up, the wood framing was done by teams of our church people who used up some of their holiday time or adjusted their schedules at the office. If they weren't inclined to use a hammer then there was always sweeping to be done, nails to be retrieved and garbage to be picked up. Coffee breaks were a chance to stand back and admire the progress, to chat with onlookers and to taste the refreshments brought by other members. Our project manager was the professional and we worked together with him. Later on, the more technical construction was taken over by the professionals as some of us nursed our blisters and admired our calluses. The awesome structure dominated the skyline on the corner and attracted a lot of attention. Now even neighbours and strangers began to look forward to its opening. Late in the fall we had a gathering of the congregation inside the empty shell. It looked huge! We were overwhelmed! Work continued inside and some helped with the painting and finishing.

The week before Christmas was extremely busy for all. Our building was finished, but the pews needed to be installed and the rug laid in the sanctuary. We also needed a general clean-up before the first of three services for Christmas Eve began at five o'clock.

Our grassroots approach to the work of building a church *and* a building once again shone through. People took time off work to help unload the shipment of pews, to sweep, vacuum, and scrub. Early Christmas Eve another team moved in to dust, wash the inside windows, and polish. My husband, our two young girls and I were part of the "last minute clean-up team." When we finished we dashed home to get dressed for the first service in our own house of worship.

Christmas Eve — the first service in our own church building! What a gift for all of us to share with the wider community!

Later, as we sat in the pews with old and new friends proudly surveying the sanctuary, our self-conscious eyes fell on the windows at the back. There is a wall of glass between the narthex and sanctuary. We suddenly became uncomfortably aware that in our washing and polishing we had missed some windows. It became a shared joke among the worshippers that we all noticed those housekeeping matters during the service. It showed our concern for what we had worked so hard to do.

The sanctuary held over 500, with space for another 200 in the adjacent narthex. That evening, over the three services, a total of 1,900 people attended. What a feeling of pride and elation!

Young people bring their friends

Following that momentous occasion, we hired another full time minister in the summer of 1989. David Kai is a diaconal minister with a soft spoken manner and a wonderful musical talent. With his guitar or at the piano, he leads children and adults in song during Junior Church or in one of his moving services. He also writes hymns and anthems and is among other musical composers in the congregation. He is a key leader of the Sunday school and the teen group called AdWOL (Adolescents Worshipping Our Lord).

We regularly count attendance at worship services. One Sunday, Tom Sherwood looked out at the children filling the front rows of Orléans United Church... and discovered that half of the little pairs of eyes watching him weren't blinking. He looked again. Each child was holding a doll, a Cabbage Patch doll. The youngest members of our congregation all sat proudly holding their own little ones. When he realized what was happening, Tom alerted the head counters for that day to count only *human* heads.

The support Tom had given us while we were grieving the death of Jamie Gosse was returned from us when his marriage ended. People who had gone through this very difficult period themselves counselled him and listened to him. Often the minister listens to everyone else but has no ear ready for him or her. We banded together as a family to help Tom and support him. Since then, love has found him again and he is happily married. He continues to lead us in thoughtful study and spiritual growth through his sermons and committee discussions. He recently earned his PhD in sociology and we celebrated with him as proudly as if we were his parents.

Yes, we do struggle just like other congregations. A number of key people felt burnt out once the building was complete and their hard work finished. Personalities got in the way temporarily of positive results. After working so hard some felt they were not needed any longer. A once small and tightly-knit group of hard workers faltered for a moment as a few dropped out. Newcomers felt they had missed out on all the excitement; some felt like outsiders. Our large mortgage is a constant strain on the budget, our wallets, and our mission.

Because our congregation is large (over 600 families), people do not get to meet new adherents as quickly as before. Often we are embarrassed to discover that a "new" family we have just introduced ourselves to have been attending for over a year. We've also had a few other problems, like break-ins, vandalism and theft. One of the furnaces needed to be replaced and the organ needed to be repaired — more money.

But even such a myriad of small problems are soon crowded out by the strong fellowship, the over-all drive and mission of the congregation.

The grassroots "ministry of every believer" feeling has grown and widened, unlike older established churches we have all experienced. If a job needs to be done, the request goes out by phone, the Sunday bulletin, the quarterly newsletter, or from the lectern during the Sunday service. In short time the call is usually answered.

The church is filled with reminders of this spirit. Before the digging began on the building site some clay was taken from the grounds and made into unique ceramic plates now used to hold the bread during communion services. The sound booth for recording the services was the inspiration of Dave Patterson, who looked after the wiring and still operates and organizes the team of people to run it each Sunday. The hymn boards, pulpit, lectern, and communion table were built and finished to match the interior by a member of the congregation and his father. The artwork for our bulletins is drawn by a young mother/artist in the congregation and sometimes by the children. We adapted the hall ourselves for better sound quality under the guidance of an internationally known acoustics expert, who is also a member of the congregation.

Whenever we feel overwhelmed by the load, someone from the congregation steps in and we realize the call we are answering is stronger than our self-doubts and frailties. Several of our members have felt the call to the ministry. Two women and one man have been ordained, and three more university students have come forward as candidates. A number of talented members of the congregation have written hymns and anthems that we use in our services. The Sunday school enrolment has reached 500. Approximately 80 volunteer teachers are involved with this "younger" congregation.

An important segment of our congregation is the youth group (AdWOL) of more than fifty 14-19 year olds. Every Sunday at both 9 and 11 a.m. they hold a special Teen Church where they tune in to the first part of the regular service and then turn off the speakers and do their own lectionary readings and discussion. AdWOL socializes once a week and has 3 weekend retreats a year. They also lead the regular worship service periodically and are especially talented in the areas of liturgical dance, drama and instrumental music.

A large junior youth group called Junior Adolescents Worshipping Our God (JAdWOG) for 11-13 year olds has also been formed, because they felt left out from the activities of the older group. This group also holds their own seminar on Sundays, based on the *Whole People of God* curriculum, and engages in regular social activities and one retreat a year. It has helped fill the gap between childhood and adulthood when the sense of belonging and worth often falter. More recently we've added a post-high school group for the "20-somethings."

Growth and success come with a price. But they're worth it.

Linda Acton-Riddle is a teacher with the Ottawa Board of Education. She is married to Gord and their daughters Erin and Carol Anne are now members of AdWOL and JAdWOG. Over the years she has served as an Elder, Sunday school superintendent, chair of the Worship Committee and a Trustee.

Highlands United Church on the mountainside in North Vancou-
ver has remained true to the vision of its founders while meeting the
future head on. The young families coming in increasing numbers
recognize that this is a place to grow and serve and they want to be
part of the action.

12

Go tell it on the mountain

by IRENE K. STRONG

When Muriel and Fred MacLeod came to the Highlands area of North Vancouver in November of 1947, they were only the 60th family to move into the area. Both veterans from Eastern Ontario, they started a lifetime of service to their church and their community.

Muriel and Fred were a formidable team. Muriel brought the same incisiveness and drive to her church and volunteer work that she displayed at the bridge table. She and Fred were part of the group that worshipped in the basements of various homes and launched their first financial campaign even before Highlands United Church was formally organized. That first fund-raising campaign raised a grand total of $85.

"We called on everybody, whether they were United Church or not," Muriel recalls. "On my first day out I managed to get only $2 after knocking on every door in my area. When I got home, I told the young pharmacy student who was boarding with us for the summer of my meagre take. Later, that young Italian Catholic boy from Ontario gave me five dollars. And then I got ten dollars from the druggist, Mr. Caspar, another Catholic. Seventeen dollars! That was nearly as much as the $18.56 we raised at our first bake sale!"

The $85 they raised, altogether, was seed money for the first hall, its addition, and parking lot and the manse, all of which were built between 1951 and 1953. The present sanctuary and Christian Education Centre followed in 1957 and 1964.

Growing a church home

The families who founded Highlands in the fall of 1948 set their roots deep in the North Shore mountainside. They turned to Presbytery for help, first in establishing a worship service in their homes; then they quickly set up a Woman's Association, a Sunday school, and a membership roll. Two years later, they had their first regular minister, a choir, and an organist. Little did they realize that by the mid '60s they would have the second largest Sunday school in Canada — 1164 children and 115 teachers. The total church membership peaked at 1024 in 1968. As they were burgeoning, they were also selecting and establishing principles that would enable Highlands to meet the eventual realities of declining enrolment, a changing community, and the need to refocus its vision.

The history of the congregation suggests that revitalization became one of the primary principles that has enabled Highlands to develop depth, stability, and relevance. As it nears the end of its first half-century of life, the congregation continues to redefine itself, balancing the needs, challenges, and strengths of its own members and of the community it serves.

The community and the people

Highlands United Church lies halfway up the mountains in North Vancouver. Although the district is part of Greater Vancouver, and is connected to Vancouver by two bridges and a sea bus, it is very much its own community, with the geography defining and informing the relationships and the people. The tree-lined rivers and creeks that pour down the mountains into the harbour, and the Trans-Canada Highway that slashes across the mountainside halfway up, divide the area into distinct neighbourhoods.

When the tract of forest known as Capilano Highlands was first opened for development following World War II, tiny Edgemont Village was the core of the existing community. It was here that Highlands United Church planted its roots.

Many of the people who came to build their homes in what was then "the bush" were war veterans. They had lived through a depression and a world war. They knew how to survive and make things happen. They longed for a stable community for their young families. Church was part of their vision — whether they were United Church or not. And their community wanted them. A real estate firm, Capilano Highlands, and two generations of the Conkey family donated four lots on which the original church and manse were built.

The people who settled around Edgemont were pioneers — suburban homesteaders — with almost overwhelming energy, commitment, and, most important, leadership skills. Their church came to be the focus of their lives. The strong sense of ownership that has prevailed through the demographic, economic, social, and personnel changes of the last 25 years can be simply stated: "This is my church, and nobody's going to take it away from me!"

The community today has an established middle-class look about it. The population decline of the first half of the '70s — when the children of the first pioneers were growing up and leaving home — has reversed itself as retiring seniors are replaced by young families and new immigrants, some from other religions, some with no religious background. The older people prefer to stay close to the Village and the services of offers but suitable accommodation is scarce.

Edgemont Village has expanded, but still retains its character. Highlands United anchors the western corner of the Village. Highlands is now one of many churches and community centres in the area, and its members come from all over the North Shore, although a core group still lives in the Highlands. While there is an expanded definition of community, there is also an attempt to re-establish the sense of neighbourhood.

Worship and work shall be one

Before there was a regular minister, a Session, or a Board of Stewards, the Building Committee was set up, and the $85 financial campaign was held. The Metropolitan Council for Church Extension approved a loan to build a church hall, and the Home Missions Board agreed to pay an ordained minister until the congregation could cover the salary itself. In 1949, the small group of worshippers that gathered in the Barracloughs' home on Sunday evenings with the Rev. H. Dickson decided to meet mid-week, each month, with half an hour for devotions, half an hour for the business of planning a new church, and a social time. The official anniversary date of the congregation goes back to a communion service held in April 1949.

Once the formal organization was in place, in January 1951, shortly after the Rev. Thomas Watson became the first regular minister, the name "Highlands United Church" was chosen, linking the church firmly to its community.

It's easy to get caught up in the energy and excitement of those first heady years when Edna and Rex Hundleby reminisce. Rex was the first Clerk of Session. He is now a trustee. Edna has filled a myriad of positions over the years.

"When we cleared the land for the first parking lot," Rex relates, "I got a load of tires to throw on the pile of trees and brush. I called the fire department, and told them not to worry if they saw a lot of smoke from out our way during the night, and then got hold of Wes Bray." Wes Bray was the minister by then. "The two of us spent the night hosing down the surrounding forest to keep the fire from getting away on us," Rex recalls, a satisfied smile crossing his face. "And when we cleared the land for the hall, several women worked right alongside us."

With the varied backgrounds of the first members, there might have been some tension as they got caught up in years of planning, fund-raising and building. "No, there weren't any problems that way," says Muriel Whitman, another pioneer with her husband Rod. "If there was any tension, it was between those who wanted to study a plan to · death before doing anything, and those who just wanted to get on with the job."

"That's right!" snaps her husband Rod. His tone leaves no doubt that he was always saying, "Let's get the show on the road!"

They had to move quickly, as people poured into the new community with their families. Hillcrest Hall was finished in October 1951. Soon they added two rooms, but that wasn't enough, so it was back to basements in homes for the overflow. Before the building was finished, Highlands had also spilled over into Highlands School, a dance studio, and even a room over the pharmacy.

When the congregation decided to build a large sanctuary with an option to add a Christian Education Centre, they chose a new site closer to Edgemont Village itself. An architect inspected the proposed site and approved it. But some wondered what could be done with a piece of land that dropped off so sharply to the creek below. To get the property ready, the creek had to be rechannelled, and thousands of yards of free fill dumped down the slope so there would be room for the CE Centre that would have to come.

It also took a lot of money. Raising that money meant further debts, canvassing, and a Wells campaign. The Wells organization, popular in those days, mounted congregational fund-raising campaigns with the precision of military manoeuvres. Their program included everything from congregational dinners to door-to-door visitations. Highlands had 266 members at the time. Those 266 members raised $100,000 in pledges, all to be paid in full within 150 weeks, over and above their existing contributions. The canvass began on April 22, 1955; the first pledge payments were due on April 30, 1955. Part of the canvass prayer states, "May we have a growing sense of the needs of our community and of our need to express our thanks and concern by giving of ourselves to all that speaks for Thee."

The people of Highlands barely had time to catch their breath after this campaign, before starting on another for the $190,000 CE Building. They also established a tradition: appeal to the congregation when special needs come up; they will respond.

Church school attendance and church membership both peaked about five years after these two buildings were completed. It's hard to imagine how the congregation ever found time to establish, staff, and maintain other church programs.

Growing activities

Eight women interested in United Church work met in March 1949 to start what many have called the backbone of Highlands. They went from being the Women's Association to the Women's Federation and then to the present United Church Women — although they did state in 1962 that, "while we had no part in drawing up this present [UCW] constitution, we are, however, guided by it and take our places as United Church Women of Canada."

Over the years, they have been involved in raising money, equipping buildings and manses, teaching Sunday school, and planning programs. But all the while, "there was time for worship, service, fun, fellowship, and work." The units originally formed around local districts, making it easy for the women to gather. But as time passed, each unit developed distinctive interests and styles as they pursued their goals and enhanced their skills. Many of the women had "little or no experience in women's work in the church, many had young families, and all had much to do in developing their own homes," says an annual UCW report from that time. The needs of the expanding congregation and church school were their focus originally, but they gradually moved into mission study and concern about the local and global communities.

And the community knew they could turn to the women's groups for help. Phyl Gibbard remembers the night shortly before Christmas, in the early '70s, when she got a phone call from a maid at a local motel, asking for help for a young Ugandan refugee family with two babies. A visit revealed that they had one suitcase for the four of them, and literally needed everything. An appeal in the church bulletin the following Sunday brought furnishings for an apartment the UCW had found, and warm clothing. One of the men helped the Ugandan husband find a job at a gas station. A UCW member provided parenting advice. The women continued to be involved with the Ugandan family for several years until they got on their feet.

Much of the incentive for making Highlands the serving church it is today came out of projects generated within the UCW — although people like the MacLeods had always brought the work of Missions and the Bible Society to the congregation. Outreach is one example. At their second meeting, in 1949, the Women's Association had a speaker from the North Vancouver District Family Welfare Bureau. By 1956, they were helping at First United Church in the downtown core of Vancouver. This is still a major congregational commitment. Also by 1956, they were assisting mental patients at Riverview Hospital, working with children with disabilities, and supporting the Christmas Bureau's food and clothing program, as well as needy local families directly.

In 1976, the UCW sponsored a craft fair to provide local artisans with a place to market their goods. They continued this service for five years until it was no longer needed.

That same year, they threw the first of Highlands' famous Flea Markets, a natural outgrowth of the rummage sales held by the Princess Anne Unit of the UCW. That first Flea Market raised $6,300, with $4,300 of that going to the Stewards for general revenue and outreach. Today the Flea Market is one of the high points of Highlands' life. While workers come from every part of the congregation for the week of the sale itself, the ongoing sorting is done by UCW members for ten months of the year. The current convenor of the market, Winnie Hamilton, is a UCW member who has been involved for years. It is rumoured there is even a 90-year-old involved, though you can't tell by looking. All of the funds raised — about $25,000 in 1993 — go to the general revenues of the church. The scope of the Flea Market goes far beyond the actual sale day. Throughout the year, clothing, furniture, and household goods go to refugees, halfway houses, and other community projects and groups.

In the early days, the UCW had a Welfare Room, which grew into the Outreach Room, and eventually became the Outreach Committee of the Unified Board when the church changed its organization in 1978. That Outreach Committee soon divided, as some of its members (several of whom had come out of Kairos, a group of senior teens and twenties) felt a greater call to global concerns and set up a Social Action Committee. Today, the two groups, along with Caring Ministry, are all under a single umbrella: H.P.H.C., "Healthy People, Healthy Community," a pilot project set up at the request of the national church. One of the objectives of this group is to forge strong connections with partners in the local and global communities.

Branching out internationally

Highlands had a head start in forming these partnerships, as members of the congregation and the ministerial staff have been supporting and serving on provincial, national, and international groups and projects for years. At last count, there were 36 people involved in different ways. For example, optometrist Duncan Tennant and his wife Dorothy have gone to the Third World many times to provide eye care and glasses with an American Christian group. Several other church members went with them at various times to assist with logistics and nursing care. While those who went looked after their own expenses, the congregation helped by supplying eyeglasses and some funds. As first-hand reports came back to the church, the people in the pews found that they could relate to the joy of a parent seeing her child for the first time. Global awareness increased.

Partnerships in Central America, which had originally been established under the Social Action Committee, were strengthened with the arrival of Don Robertson as minister. Don had visited refugee camps in Central America prior to coming to Highlands, and had served as a resource person to the local group. As the scope of outreach work grew and became more ecumenical through involvement with Project Ploughshares, Ten Days For World Development, and the Christian Task Force on Central America, connections were strengthened further. The speed with which a response to the Chiapas rebellion in Mexico, following the elections there, was initiated showed the effectiveness of the whole network.

When the Social Action Committee was started in the late '70s, it chose education as the way to achieve its goal of looking at global issues from a Christian perspective. Groups that work this way have a hard time seeing and demonstrating their results. Jon Carrodus, who with his wife Simone has been a driving force from the beginning, recalls the discussion around Highlands' first participation in Walk for Peace. They weren't sure if they should even put it into the Sunday bulletin! Several years later, in promoting World Food Day, the minister at the time agreed to preach on the politics of food distribution around the world. Jon grins as he recalls how his Social Action Committee dramatized the message: "I don't think anyone will ever forget Ed Peterson scurrying down the aisle with a shopping cart in the middle of the sermon." The group has made extremely effective use of various means of communication in the church — from bulletins to announcements from the pulpit, from special events to the sale of projects directly related to their objectives. It is no coincidence that Rigoberto Menchu, winner of the Nobel Prize for Peace, spent several months with the Carrodus family while studying English.

Highlands involvement in refugee sponsorship goes back to August 1979, when Jean Gabrielse, after watching the plight of the Vietnamese "Boat People" on TV, called the chair of the board. The board quickly gave unanimous approval from a hastily-called quorum for Highlands to sponsor the first family — who actually turned out to be three families with the same name, Nguyen. Three months later, they arrived. Six months after that, they were self-supporting. A Refugee Committee was set up, answerable to the board but funded under its own budget with gifts from he congregation. Jean and Mirv Harper have been with the committee since its inception. They have sponsored over 60 refugees from nearly all the hot spots around the world, and assisted about 100 more. Between 1979 and 1993, they spent $123,050 in helping refugees. They have helped newcomers settle in, been advocates for others, and kept the concerns of the world's homeless before the congregation.

The Refugee Committee represents one of the strengths of this congregation. There is a climate operating at Highlands that spawns both ad hoc and longer-term groups and activities. If they are able to support themselves, and have goals consistent with Highlands' own, they have access to a meeting place, a communications network, and assistance of the ministerial staff in getting their programs going. Often, these new groups attract people from outside the church, too.

One of the problems, of course, is that they often act independently. Maintaining a satisfactory balance requires patience and respect on the part of the group and of the board. A lot of initiative and creativity has been generated by individuals choosing to work this way.

Children, youth, and intergenerational ministry

There has always been a place for children and youth at Highlands. Even in the early days, they came to church school in such numbers that there was even the suggestion that the church not accept one more child! Instead, however, the church moved to two sessions. At one point, it even used the stairwells as classrooms, according to Doree Piercy. While her husband Dick was church school superintendent, Doree was one who had to teach in the stairwells.

There were Hi-C, Explorers and CGIT groups. A long association with Scouting began in 1962, and expanded to include the full range of Scout and Guide activities. Scouts are, however, the only mid-week group that survived the great decline in children and youth participation that has afflicted not only Highlands, but most mainline Protestant churches. Highlands church school continued, but the numbers dropped dramatically. For almost 20 years there has been an ongoing effort to create structures, programs, and leadership that would appeal to children, youth, and young adults. The congregation backed their commitment with additional funding. Youth groups ebbed and flowed, but gradually a small core emerged, some of whom were second-generation Highlanders.

When Don Robertson came to the church as senior minister in 1985, he helped set in place a process of planning for the future. With his support, the congregation and official board developed a vision of genuine community — one in which at least three generations are in dynamic and faithful relatedness with each other. Highlands certainly had the three generations. The culmination of this intentional effort came in 1987 when Ross and Jeannie White were called to join Don, to expand the Family Ministry, and to be deliberate about viewing the congregation in generational terms. The ministerial team set out to create a youth program that was more than just a youth group, by increasing youth participation in every aspect of church life.

Ross, who has also been chair of the Conference Ministry with Children working unit, outlines some of their strategies: "We had to diversify so we would appeal to a larger group of kids, not just those who were joiners. We brought a Tentmaker, a student intern leader, from Naramata, spearheaded a Vacation Bible School that included Anglicans, Lutherans, and another United Church nearby, and ran a peer counselling course. We had to spread the ownership around — in worship, the board, the committees. We put liaison people with each sector where youth are involved."

The ministry of music

The largest group of youth in the church when the Family Ministry got underway was Genesis Too, a choir started by Gillian Irwin in the fall of 1984. When she was hired to lead an existing choir of young adults, today's Spirit Singers, she asked if she could start one for youth as well. Since music had always been an integral part of the church, even before they had a formal meeting place, nobody was going to say no. Many people around remembered the 80-voice Sunday school choir of the late '60s. "Gillian was an answer to my prayers," says Muriel Whitman, founder of the first children's choir 40 years ago. "I had always hoped that someone with my love of music but with more knowledge would come along and take the kids on."

Gillian herself feels that the timing was right. There was a chain reaction of people willing to do something new. The original youth, from Grade 3 (old enough to read) to Grade 12, were from church families. But they make up only half of the group of 73 singers today. Both Gillian's choirs — Genesis Too and the Spirit Singers — operate on the same principles: fun, a sense of community, being vital to worship and the church, and making a difference when they're there. They present a worship service each year, and then take that service to another community.

When asked how she decides what Genesis Too is going to sing, Gillian explains: "The message has to be right for the kids, simple and straightforward. It has to be about friendship, serving, supporting each other — about what God wants them to do. And I don't use songs written for children!"

After Genesis Too has sung its anthem, it will usually stay for the time with children. Then, with a few exceptions, its members join a church school class. Although the choir sings twice a month, an increasing number of the youth also attend the classes on the alternate Sundays when they aren't singing.

Some of her members come from God's Free Spirits, pre-schoolers led by Gillian's sister-in-law Cheryl.

In addition, there is the Chancel Choir, mainly seniors, who have been singing at the second worship service for many years. Their Food Bank concert usually raises about $2,000. "This is a choir-crazy church," laughs Geordie Roberts, their director, who has recently started working with the Revelation Choir, made up of senior teens and young adults.

Music fits the intergenerational model in the church's vision, though the choice of music and instruments doesn't always fit the stereotypes for the ages. The Chancel Choir can swing as well as any of them. There are about 175 singers in the five choirs today. Music brought many of them to the church.

Worship — the sign of the community

Worship services are more than a gathering of the people. They are designed to reflect what Highlands is, does, and dreams of.

Jeannie White says that after she preaches, there is an increase in the number of women who come in for counselling. "Having a woman's voice at the front gives them permission to ask for what they need," she says. "They see that they have a right to ask."

When it became church policy for children to participate in communion, Jeannie remembers, work had to be done. "We had a lot of educating to do with parents and kids, ushers and servers, the Worship Committee and the board. and we had to use language that helps adults understand what it means to have kids at communion." Debbie Bowman, a candidate for ministry from Highlands, prepared a list of worship and church language that is hard for newcomers to relate to, and provided more relevant terms. "We use this in many ways," says Ross. "It's just one more example of how we try to make people feel comfortable here."

In addition to the Worship Committee, there is a Chancel Group, a Music Committee, and Ushering, Communion, Lay Reading, and Baptism co-ordinators. The whole Worship Committee, in co-operation with the ministerial staff, is constantly looking for creative, meaningful ways to enhance worship and make it more accessible to children and to the numbers of new members who come from different religious backgrounds or from none at all.

When the Scouting and Guiding movement have their annual church parade and the children and youth march in to the skirl of the bagpipes, they and their leaders take part in every facet of the service. The message is focused on their needs, in language appropriate to their experiences.

Feeling comfortable and welcome at worship, and having their children feel the same way, is one of the major reasons that many have for choosing Highlands as their church, say those who have "shopped around."

Over the top and part way down the other side

The numerical growth that Highlands experienced in its first 20 years left the congregation unprepared for what followed. The initial euphoria helped carry people through just about everything — money, planning, canvassing, building, staffing, learning, and just plain coping.

Once the plateau was reached, there were only a few short years to try to assimilate the significance of all that had gone before and to learn from it. Once the decline started, it was so ongoing that even the knowledge it wasn't only a local phenomenon couldn't hide the disappointment.

But a paradox emerges when talking to people who have come to Highlands within the last 20 years, usually from churches in the same situation. They remember that even then, Highlands had a vitality and sense of purpose that attracted them. The numbers may have been down, but the congregation was willing to get on with the work of being the church.

When the Unified Board replaced the traditional Stewards and Session in 1978, a series of adaptations followed. Some feel that in addition to enhancing the power of the laity, this change also marked a subtle shift in the roles of the ministers. With strong lay leadership at Highlands, a three-pronged triangular structure emerged — though not on paper. There appears to be a delicate balancing act in place, with the official board in one corner, the ministerial staff in another, and the various groups and individuals that spring up, and usually operate under the umbrella of the board but with separate funding, in the third. The fact that this unofficial structure has managed to work at all is due to the sensitivity and respect the three groups accord to each other, but it hasn't always been easy. This unofficial arrangement is an illustration of the "creative tension" that keeps Highlands vibrant.

The board has made further changes to its structure recently, in an effort to flatten it and cut down on meetings. All committees now meet on the same night as the official board itself. Theological reflections, an attempt to relate the work of the board to Highlands' calling to be the Church of Christ, are given by either the board chair or by one of the ministers.

Over the years, Highlands has had to make many difficult decisions, and wasn't afraid to make them. Sometimes there was the luxury of time to go through an extensive planning process. Other decisions required immediate action. In most cases, the decisions seem to have been the right ones — but not always. The congregation appears to adhere to Lester Pearson's adage: "Don't be afraid to make an honest mistake."

The Christian Education Centre that once resonated with church-based programs is now a community meeting place as well. Upkeep became more difficult; many who came had no sense that this was their place. There were an incredible variety of groups using the Centre. For several years, the Muslims gathered there on Saturdays, using the kitchen as well as the auditorium. When the Sweet Adelines barbershop singing group were practising, Dog Obedience classes had to go into the far corner. All this leasing, renting, scheduling of space, and collecting the donations required additional volunteer time, and monitors still had to be on duty five nights a week.

The congregation was on a new journey, and there were few guideposts along the way.

One reason Highlands has come through this transition time so well has been the presence of those who can be called maintainers and sustainers. Mainly retired, usually long-time members, they have kept the plant operating, often on limited funds. They can also be found helping with administrative tasks. But the most important thing they have cared for over the years is the vision on which Highlands was founded — a vision that has been shared, restated and redefined, but never lost.

Highlands today

Highlands' physical plant is basically the same as it was when the Christian Education Centre was finished, in 1964. A small chapel has been built behind the sanctuary. A Memorial Garden, at the back of the church, lies at the edge of the ravine. Inside the church, a well-stocked and well-used library with a Children's Memorial Library has been added over the years, with help from the UCW. The grand piano in the sanctuary, paid for by a special appeal in the early '90s, enhances an already rich music program.

As the church neared its 40th anniversary, it became apparent that major repairs and upgrading were needed in many areas. Completing them seemed to be an appropriate way to celebrate the anniversary. A congregation-wide project, Vision 40, raised the needed funds: $140,000 was pledged over the five year project, and an extra $4,000 was actually collected. It was the largest campaign held since the mid-'60s.

The congregation has a large number of retirees, many of them in the category of senior-seniors. They are incredibly self-sufficient, run their own programs, and take good care of one another. Many attend the early worship service because that's where the children are. Young families continue to return to Highlands, attracted by the music, worship, learning opportunities, relevance — and energy. They are a driving force in beautifying the front of the church so it will present a more welcoming image to the community.

Pat Bell, chair of the Official Board, and minister Don Robertson, interviewed in early 1994, both wondered where the volunteers and funds were going to come from to continue the work at Highlands. Like many others, they expressed a concern that an integral aspect of church life would be lost if more and more of the work was done by salaried people.

Highlands didn't have time to do any more wondering as Don left for another congregation. Interim minister the Rev. Cheryl Black came for a year — and what a year it turned out to be! The ministerial staff, board and congregation engaged in a lengthy, extensive evaluation and visioning process in the midst of which Ross went on educational leave. But our student intern helped carry out the work successfully, demonstrating again Highland's flexibility.

A 17-member pastoral relations committee, which included everyone who wanted to serve on it, was engaged in its work at the same time. The visioning process played a key role in the call to the Rev. Deborah Laing to join Ross and Jeannie White and the congregation in ministry at Highlands. In the midst of all this, givings, attendance and the work of the congregation continued.

When Deborah arrived with her husband and infant son, she quickly revealed the strengths that had lead to her call: solid preaching, a respect for lay leadership, an ability to relate to all generations and a depth and flexibility that come from ministries in Saskatchewan, Sherbrooke, Quebec and Chicago.

In her first sermon at Highlands, Deborah said she had been sent from Chicago with a commission from an African-American grandmother: "You go tell them the good news about Jesus—and *keep on telling them*." That's what Deborah and Highlands will keep on doing from the mountainside in North Vancouver.

What has Highlands learned in the process?

The ups and downs of Highlands' history sometimes seem to mirror the peaks and slopes of the North Shore mountains. What have we learned from our experiences? Perhaps these thoughts might be helpful to other congregations as they deal with either growth or decline:

- Have a vision, set manageable goals, and put a process in place to review them.
- Think about how you measure success. Appreciate that some projects and processes take more time than others.
- Maintain strong ties with the local community and the wider church. Try to include all gifts in worship and all other applicable areas.
- Create a climate that encourages creativity and initiative, and then be prepared to be flexible.
- Deal with difficult and contentious matters when they come up. Focus on process, so that polarization is kept to a minimum.
- Offer a worship experience that is inclusive, relevant, and centred in the scriptures.
- Take extra care with what seem to be small things — welcoming and saying thank you, having good signs around for those unfamiliar with the building.
- Support those who are placed in the position of having to make decisions in a hurry.
- Recognize that some programs are born to die, but it's hard to let go. Receiving acknowledgement for what you have done makes it easier to let go, as does an ongoing evaluation process.
- Know your congregation. Know the age groups, family situations, strengths, needs. Update your information regularly.
- Keep up with technology, and learn to use it to your advantage.
- Provide those who are planning to serve in the ordained or lay ministry with practical learning experiences and a chance to share their gifts.
- Look for opportunities for giving outside the regular budget.
- Set processes in place that incorporate planning for the future.
- Vary your program for content, time, and length, so people have more opportunities to take part. Consider child care for young families and transportation for seniors.
- Celebrate as often as you can.

Irene K. Strong is a retired ESL instructor, mother of three, and, with husband Irv, a life-long learner, music lover, world traveller and sometime fisherman. Her chief areas of interest in the church are worship, adult education and working with the books at the Flea Market.

Woodcliff United in Calgary learned first hand the benefits of hiring competent consultants to direct a stewardship program to pay off the costs of a major renovation.

No free lunch

by ROBERT MUTLOW

In the midst of our church renovation campaign in the fall of 1989, an invitation to attend a free lunch arrived on my desk. A stewardship consulting company wanted to meet with pastors and finance committee chairs to offer their fund-raising services.

I phoned up Brent Rusk, our Finance Committee chair. I suggested we take in this free lunch. His response was "Bob, there are no free lunches."

Half a decade later, I can agree with him. It wasn't a free lunch — but it was certainly the most important church meal I have ever attended.

I was called to Woodcliff United in July of 1988. Woodcliff was, in many ways, very much like the church I had previously served in Winnipeg. It was part of that huge building boom of the late 1950s.

The Rev. Howey, the assistant minister of St. Matthew's United, a neighbouring church, did the leg work to get Woodcliff going in this burgeoning new area of Calgary. At the Thanksgiving service of 1956 held in the local Spruce Cliff School, Howey offered some realistic advice:

> You and I have left home and other churches in other parts of the world. We are going to build a new community here. The homes are being built, the lawns seeded, children are going to school. But we have

no churches. We know that with God's help we can build these churches and it will be done. But there are going to be moments when we are going to wonder how we can get enough money, moments when we will wonder why people will not help like they could and should, moments of discouragement, and moments of anger and conflict.

In spite of his cautionary tone — or perhaps because of it — the church-building movement took off. In December 1960, a fine brick Christian Education Building was dedicated. There were so many children in the area, a multi-purpose space was more important than a sanctuary. The sanctuary could come later.

Adjusting to changing times

However, by the late '60s and early '70s, church building fell out of favour. The emphasis shifted to programs and people rather than buildings. Woodcliff — under the leadership of the Rev. Norman Hunter, a Methodist Pastor who came to Canada from England — had a creative and lively presence in the west end of Calgary. In the liturgical ferment of the '60s, the flexibility of their space allowed them to do a lot of experimenting with worship forms. Norman Hunter served Woodcliff United for 22 years of very effective ministry before retiring. Naturally, it was very difficult for someone to follow him. So the next few years were transition years. When I arrived in 1988 the congregation was ready to move in new directions. And move we did!

In the 1980s, new neighbourhoods were growing by leaps and bounds across a major freeway from the church. These were communities built with fine homes and big expectations by baby boomers. Worship in a gymnasium on steel chairs and Sunday school facilities that needed upgrading weren't going to "cut it" with this group. A feeling began to grow in the Woodcliff Church community that something dramatic needed to be done.

The interviews with prospective ministers for the congregation included a good deal of discussion of where Woodcliff was going. I recall having breakfast with Sylvia Teare, the chair of the pastoral relations committee, a relative newcomer to the church, and Greta Thompson, a long-time member, the morning after an interview. Over muffins and coffee, we wrestled with Woodcliff's options and how to bring to fruition the dream of a sanctuary.

Woodcliff had already had a committee to determine the cost of erecting a sanctuary. Graham Paynter, a young man who had grown up in the church, chaired the committee and really wanted to see something happen.

When they reported to the congregation in March of 1987 they were asked to explore other alternatives because of the prohibitive costs of construction. The congregation could barely meet its regular, ongoing expenses. It didn't feel it could commit itself to a massive new debt.

Woodcliff decides to renovate, not build

In the fall of 1988, Woodcliff established a new committee to recommend whether to build a new sanctuary or to renovate the present facilities. Steve Crosby, a Maritimer who had moved to Calgary during the oil boom, agreed to chair this group, which was carefully made up of newcomers and long-time members. After looking at the demographics, the financial history of the church, and trying to plot the growth trends, the Committee recommended, on May 31, 1989, to "redevelop the facilities." Rather than building a new sanctuary, Woodcliff decided to renovate the 1960 gymnasium into a multi-purpose worship facility, and to up-grade the Sunday school facilities. In the fall of that year an architectural firm with a well-deserved reputation for bringing church buildings in on budget was chosen to redesign the building for the '90s.

The architects started by refiguring the gymnasium. Seating was arranged in a semi-circle, creating a stronger sense of community. The chancel area was given a dramatic look by a new raised ceiling and a curved, wood-panelled facade. The foyer and sanctuary were carpeted in grey. Comfortable sanctuary chairs in a green shade added to a contemporary feel. A huge new window enabled us to appreciate adjacent Edworthy park; as church growth specialist George Hunter has noted: "Growing churches tend to feel connected to the outdoors." Now as we move through the church year we can watch the changing seasons out of this marvellous western window. Windows and doors in the lower hall created a welcoming space for the Sunday school. A new kitchen with modern facilities and dishwasher was added to the lower hall, and this became our Sunday morning coffee space and banquet space during the week.

Paying the piper

In the meantime, the members of the Finance Committee were sweating. How were these changes to be paid for?

That was when the invitation to attend the free lunch arrived. It was an unprecedented offer. There hadn't been such an invitation before, or since, to such an event. For Woodcliff, the moment was propitious.

The Finance Committee wrestled with the question: Did we want to pay an outsider to help us do our funding? The realization grew that as we hired architects to plan the building we needed outside expertise to help us pay for it. As one of the older members of the Finance Committee said, "We'll only get one kick at this can. We had better do this right."

David Jackson came from Denver, Colorado to work with us. David was a very suitable choice. He was willing to be sensitive to the Canadian ethos, to use inclusive language, and to adapt the fund-raising program for our United Church needs.

Employing a stewardship consultant for a set fee regardless of the outcome took a lot of the pressure off the process. We were hiring a consultant who had the expertise to organize us. As an outsider, he could push and prod us as an outsider in ways that none of us insiders would even consider.

Any church considering using a stewardship consultant needs to promote the idea to their people on the basis that the church is hiring a staff person with expertise for a particular function. That person does not do the work; the congregation does it. The stewardship person is the facilitator and organizer.

The cold hard reality is that you need to spend money to raise money. Yet the process has all kinds of good spin-offs in terms of community building and a renewed sense of purpose.

One of the things David made very clear was that we needed to follow the plan. There could be no short cuts. The theme of the campaign was "Not Equal Giving But Equal Sacrifice." Everyone in the congregation would be asked to make some lifestyle change so that they could make a substantial three year pledge over and above regular givings. To make that happen, over 130 people were involved in a huge organizational structure that we called "Woodcliff 2000."

The actual stewardship campaign began with "Kick-Off Sunday" on March 17, 1989. It ended with a Congregational Banquet and Celebration Service on June 3, 1989. At that service, Woodcliff 2000 chair Brent Rusk recalled that free lunch and announced that $566,000 had been pledged over the coming three year period. By the first Sunday of June in 1993, the third anniversary of the Woodcliff 2000 campaign, $506,000 had been contributed. This enabled the congregation to burn the bank mortgage at a celebration for all ages at Elkanna Ranch. In the final year of the campaign, 1993, $60,592 was given to Woodcliff 2000 over and above regular givings. We still have $12,000 in our Redevelopment Account, and some outstanding pledges are still coming in.

The pyramid process

The program works on a pyramid model of giving. Consultant David Jackson sat down with some of the core people, including myself as minister, to choose a Steering Committee of 19 households. This group was to be made up of dedicated church members who had credibility and who could make a substantial contribution to the campaign in order to inspire others to give also. Each of these households was assigned an area of responsibility. Brent Rusk agreed to act as Campaign Director, along with his wife Joan. Brent had been recruited to the Finance Committee by a former chair of the board, who realized that if anything was going to happen at Woodcliff, it needed dynamic new leadership. Brent brought the kind of enthusiasm and drive that make things happen. The campaign directors and pastor were to set the standard for responsible leadership of the program. The director was to model the priority of the program by giving it "all out" time commitment, to speak positively and enthusiastically.

The stewardship consultant, David Jackson, developed a set of manuals for each position. These were clearly laid out and adapted for our congregation. He organized a variety of meetings to orient people to their area of responsibility, and flew to Calgary from Denver on a regular basis to monitor the progress of the campaign.

As a sample of how the Manuals operated, here is the Campaign Director's job description:
- give leadership to the Steering Committee,
- work in partnership with the Pastor to see that the plans of the campaign were followed and the calendar adhered to closely,
- provide liaison with the Consultant to see the work was completed,
- act as the official spokesperson for the campaign,
- make a sacrificial commitment early in the campaign.

These were fleshed out with a time chart so that the Director could be sure the campaign was on track.

An essential component of the stewardship program was a home visitation of everyone in the congregation. The purpose of this visit was to discuss, positively, the church and its ministries, its plans for the future work and its members' dreams. No money would be asked for at this visit. However, visitors would encourage households to begin thinking of how they could contribute. An older couple, Tom and Bernice Humphrey, and a younger couple, Graham and Elizabeth Paynter, all well known in the congregation, were recruited to the Steering Committee to select and train the visitors with the help of the Consultant.

Marlene & Mark Podwysocki were named secretaries of the campaign. Marlene had been the church secretary at Woodcliff and knew many of the people; Mark had been involved in Sunday school and administration. They were responsible for the master lists, the mailings, and pledge cards.

An essential — and perhaps unexpected — component was the prayer team of Gerry Scharff and Barbara Hatfield. Part of their responsibility was organizing an "All Night Prayer Vigil." Each of these women brought a unique background to this part of the campaign. Barbara was a kindergarten teacher who had worked as a Christian Education director. Gerry Scharff was enrolled in the St. Stephen's College field-based Diaconal Program. She was doing her training program in our congregation and had done a lot of work in Christian Education and Pastoral Care. These two women agreed to organize the "All Night Prayer Vigil" although, along with the rest of us, they weren't sure how it would "fly" in a United Church. With the assistance of the Sunday school they made up a 24-hour Prayer Wheel and invited people to sign up for one hour. Over 70 people participated.

There was a special feeling in the room that night. People shared, prayed, sang, meditated, discussed, or reflected in silence. Common responses afterward included comments like these:

- one hour was not adequate,
- the presence of God was real,
- we could feel the energy,
- we came in spite of some trepidation and found there were benefits to praying in community.

The 24-hour unbroken prayer chain was a powerful expression of our love for God. One of the real lessons of the campaign was that it was important to do everything the campaign called for — not to modify it to make it comfortable. The all night prayer vigil turned out to be one of the highlights of the campaign.

Barbara and Gerry also involved the children in a variety of ways in the campaign. However, one of our regrets was that we didn't put more emphasis on the youth and children's component.

Promotion was essential. Charlene Baker, a super organizer, and Ken Teare, a computers whiz, did a super job in getting the word out. Special letterhead was printed up. For the seven weeks of the campaign a weekly householder mailing was sent out to keep people informed on the progress of the campaign. These were professionally printed, using pictures and other appealing techniques. Themes of the newsletters focused on "Involvement," "What is Woodcliff 2000?" "An Opportunity & A Challenge," "24 Hour Prayer Vigil — Powerful Success," "If We Want it to Happen it Will Happen," and "Thank You to the People of Woodcliff." The last newsletter announced the amount pledged. So the title read, "$566,000 Out of This World!!!"

Spreading the commitment

The Brocks and Hatfields, both long time members of the congregation, organized an Advance Commitment Dinner. This was a fun dinner at
the church with Wendy's chilli and an icebreaker using children's building
blocks. At the dinner, Dr. Bruce Hatfield, a well-known Calgary doctor,
gave his endorsement to the campaign. Bruce, who has given years of leadership to the city and church on issues of sexuality, life, and death, agreed
that it was time to make the move. Woodcliff had emphasized programs
over buildings in the past, he said, but it was now time to do something
about the building.

Walter Brock, who had lots of church and political fund-raising experience, brought much practical experience to the process. Kaye Brock,
whose great aunt, Henrietta Muir-Edwards, had been part of the "Famous
Five" Alberta group that got women declared as persons in the Canadian
legal system, played a key role as part of the architect's planning committee. Kathleen Hatfield brought her insights and her ability to get things
done.

The Advance Commitment Dinner also involved George and Bonnie
Edworthy, whose family had given the land for the original building. Taken
all together, it was a great success, probably the most fun event of the campaign.

Setting a good example

The Steering Committee members were asked to make an initial pledge
in the first week of the campaign. In the pyramid model of giving the Steering Committee was expected to raise a third of the goal, the Advance Commitment Dinner the next third, and the Banquet the remaining third. Each
group was to set a model for and to excite the next group. With great anticipation, those of us in that Steering Group pencilled our pledges. According to campaign expectations, these pledges should reflect a lifestyle
change to make it happen.

The 19 households pledged only $55,000. Consultant David Jackson
was really despondent. He said, "This isn't going to fly. Maybe we had
better cancel the campaign." We needed at least $100,000!

I can still feel the sense of disappointment as we sat around the church
lounge hearing that bombshell. We talked, and wrestled, and then decided
that it was too soon to call it quits.

So we went back to the Steering Committee of 19 households and said,
"Let's sharpen our pencils again. What we have committed won't model
sacrificial giving to the Advance Commitment Dinner or the Banquet. We
need to raise one-third of our goal!"

The response this time was terrific. $120,000 was pledged from that group. We knew then we were sailing.

Each of the Steering Group then recruited church folk to be part of their committee. This involved about 60 more persons. This group was invited to come to the Advance Commitment Dinner to make their pledge. The Steering Committee's amount was announced and this second group was challenged. They pledged double the Steering Committee!

Brent Rusk and Walter Brock suddenly had a new challenge: what if the rest of the congregation would feel they didn't have to do anything? Enough had already been raised!

Everyone was invited to a Congregational Banquet. Four couples took on the mammoth task of organizing the banquet and an accompanying children's event. A special program was offered for children at a different spot. Over 300 people attended the banquet. A special effort was made to make the banquet a warm and wonderful evening with a fun program by the choir. Pledge Cards were passed out to be returned then or on the following Sunday. People who had special resources were visited individually and invited to make a special gift.

By then the campaign had taken on a life of its own. People wanted to be part of it. The pledges rolled in, and kept coming after the close of the campaign.

Collecting the pledges

A vital component to making the program successful was the Follow-Up Committee. This committee was co-chaired by long time members Greta and Herb Thompson who had a lot of credibility in the congregation. Their committee met monthly for three years. They organized welcoming events for newcomers, such as special coffee fellowships after church or Spaghetti dinners. During these events, the programs at the church were highlighted and newcomers were invited to become part of Woodcliff 2000. Special anniversary events were held each year, culminating with the fun family afternoon and barbecue supper at Elkanna Ranch. Newsletters were mailed regularly. A giant jigsaw puzzle of the church was on display at worship with a new piece added to the puzzle every time $26,000 was collected. A designated person worked with people who fell behind in their pledges for whatever reason.

In the end, the committee had such a good time working together they hated to disband. This campaign was a real highlight for the over 130 people involved. The process was a community builder. Most households were visited; people who had never met before planned, laughed, and prayed together.

David Jackson kept in touch with us over the three years. We got written up in one of his bulletins for our Puzzle Promotion. His encouragement and suggestions were more than helpful. We could not have done this program without the services of a stewardship consultant. David Jackson provided organizational direction that has worked time and time again. He organized us, supported us, and challenged us as only an outsider with expertise can.

The challenge to think big

The challenge in such a situation is to think big and act big. We need never be apologetic about asking for money again. There is a real joy in giving. People deserve to have that opportunity.

Accountability has grown in our community. We learned how to talk about what we were prepared to give. People shared from the pulpit the kinds of lifestyle changes they were making to make their contribution to the campaign. Some of those changes included:
• postponing a summer vacation
• offering child care to the congregation
• re-arranging retirement plans
• giving up some meals out
• making a substantial one-time gift to the church over and above regular givings. These ranged from $5000 to $25,000.

In such discussion and sharing, our accountability grows with each other and God. In any future stewardship campaign I would want to build in this component of discussing how much we are prepared to give and what kind of lifestyle changes we are considering. We need to talk with each other and to reflect prayerfully about our stewardship.

Church building promotes growth in every way. It helps to incorporate new people. It attracts newcomers who want to be part of a growing, changing community. It empowers long-time members with new sense of purpose and passion.

I believe it was more than coincidence that the lunch invitation arrived on my desk just when we needed help. God provides in many ways. There was a certain sense that the "time was right for this project" and it took wings and flew in ways that most of us never dreamed of. It was some free lunch!

The Reverend Robert Mutlow is married to Katie Hildebrandt, a registered dietician. They have two children, Sean and Natasha. Robert was ordained in 1971 and has served in the three prairie provinces.

Congregational renewal is not necessarily tied to building pro-grams. Deer Lake United in Burnaby, B.C. liked being a small church; they just didn't want to isolate themselves from their neighbourhood.

14

*A*ffirming what we are

by DAVID MARTYN

In 1990, Deer Lake United decided to participate in a Congregational Vitalization Program put on by the Centre for the Study of Church in Ministry, based at the Vancouver School of Theology. The program involved many lay groups, plus a Pastor's Group for the clergy of the five participating churches.

Our reason for deciding to participate was simple. We felt the need for a structured and accountable process to enable us to plan our future life together. So, with Bud Phillips and Marion Best leading us, we began an 18-month, 4-phase program.

The first phase, "The Past in Our Future," allowed members of the congregation to examine significant historical moments, decisions, contextual developments, and the ethos that brought us to the present moment. This process involved digging up — and living through again — the painful memories associated with a forced amalgamation of three congregations, 20 years before. But it also allowed us to bury those memories with reverence rather than avoidance.

When we started the Vitalization Program we were called Central Burnaby United Church — an amalgamation of three congregations:

St. Matthew's, which began in a local school in 1959 as a satellite Sunday School of West Burnaby United Church; Douglas Road, which began in 1927 and became part of a three-point charge with two congregations in North Burnaby; and Deer Lake, which began in 1924 and became part of a two-point charge with East Burnaby United Church.

For the congregations of Deer Lake and Douglas Road there were still memories of the depression that came soon after their formation. In the 1930s, Burnaby was a place where the "poor folks" lived — those who could not afford to live in the cities of Vancouver or New Westminster.

St. Matthew's began during the advent of the great Sunday school expansion of the early sixties and the suburbanization of Burnaby. Each of the churches became single-point charges with a minister to call their own during a time when churches were built in each neighbourhood so that anyone who needed to walk to church could do so. But the growth of population in Burnaby in the 1960s did not mean that their was to be a corresponding growth in the size of the United Churches; instead there was an increase in the number of denominations. When the anticipated growth did not occur, these three single pastoral charges could not survive on their own.

Although there were memories that the Presbytery had forced the amalgamations, the reality was that the Presbytery helped the congregations to survive.

The Vitalization program helped us to retell this story and let go of some residual anger that was still present. Although the plan was to sell all three churches and build a new one, that never happened. The newly amalgamated congregation moved into the Deer Lake building and, as property prices rose, could not afford a new property. The proceeds from the sale of the other two buildings were used instead to pay off loans and renovate the Deer Lake building, now named Central Burnaby United Church.

Although the plan was to take three small congregations and make a larger one, the reality was the three small churches became one small church. It remained small because all the people from the three small churches wanted to be in a small church. Although it was small, it was stronger — the people who remained really wanted to be there.

"The Past in Our Future" phase involved congregational interviews by members who were trained to listen and record information that would help us know four different aspects of our corporate history: Lived Moments, Manifestos, Comparative Psycho-History and Sagas.

Lived Moments are those moments in our lives when we are aware that something is forming or being formed in us that is much richer, wider, and more universal than the meaning of that moment itself. It may be an incident, a verbal or non-verbal exchange in a relationship, or a conscious awareness of the coming together of events, persons and life-time. We may feel it is important enough at the time, but when seen in retrospect, we recognize that moment helped to determine and form our personality.

One member spoke of a difficult family time in the 1950s. "Everything seemed to be falling apart in my life, but the church was there, never judging, silently and actively supportive. It's home for me and I am part of it, I always will be."

Manifestos are descriptive statements that recall when an individual stood for something, even when taking that particular stand meant some personal risk. A manifesto is a decision that defines the person or group who makes it.

During the United Church Ventures in Mission Program to raise $25 million for new church work, Central Burnaby did not participate and there was some guilt about their lack of action. So in 1988, when a number of congregations were decreasing their givings to the Mission and Service Fund, this congregation decided to support it even more and givings increased 10% that year. The congregation's manifesto was "we are part of The United Church of Canada and proud of it."

Decisions are always made in context. That context can be seen as the "comparative psycho-history." By examining the cultural and community conditions under which we made decisions, we discovered how our history affected our current process. The Douglas Road and Deer Lake congregations were formed by the "dirty '30's." Even though many in the congregation were very young then, the corporate identity of the congregation was still strongly influenced by attitudes and cautions that were deeply embedded in the founding members of the church during those difficult years. The members of St. Matthew's, on the other hand, reflected the optimism and expectancy of the '50s.

Sagas are the themes that describe us. These themes are a movement beyond simple storytelling to identify themes that tie together the collective life of the congregation. They may be majestic or humble, complicated or simple threads that run through the years. Central

Burnaby would say "we are a church for young families" and then note that, in general, the minister of the church had always been a young person with children. They would also say "we are the church no one can find." Both of these sagas would be addressed later in the program.

The dominant stories told of a caring community that included people with broken lives and broken hearts; it helped us recognize that our current experiences of caring were part of a long tradition of a small, caring, community church.

The second phase, "The Church in Community and Context," brought the sociologists and statisticians in the congregation out of the woodwork. A survey was done of every congregational member and then this data was compared with Canadian census data for our defined neighbourhood. We discovered that our church had a lower percentage of people under 35 than the neighbourhood. Our congregation was 66% female, 34% male, compared to 52% female, 48% male in the neighbourhood. More of the congregation was married or widowed, and significantly fewer of the congregation were single when compared to the neighbourhood. More than 50% attended a United Church when they were ten years old, the balance came from a wide range of Christian backgrounds. More than half grew up in the city or suburbs. Roughly 65% had attended Central Burnaby for less than ten years, but 78% had attended some United Church for more than ten years. Most came to Central Burnaby because it was close to where they lived. Our congregation was slightly better educated than the neighbourhood. Two-thirds of the congregation had post-secondary education versus about half for the neighbourhood. Significantly more of the congregation worked in the health and education fields than the general population; significantly fewer in administration and sales.

We discovered that we were basically middle-aged baby boomers. Our average age was 41 — the same as the minister; we had few people with either low or high incomes. We discovered that we had a congregation that felt good about itself, except in two areas: youth ministry and adult education.

The third phase, "Exploring the Assumptions of Faith," involved large numbers of the congregation in discovery groups. These groups looked at such topics as the mission of the church, the meaning of the gospel, and the nature of ministry. We used the study book *Of Bodies, Priests and Stewards*, by Brian Fraser, which was written for the Centre for Study of Church and Ministry.

In the first two phases, in dialogue with the other participating churches, we noted that each congregation had experienced moments when it felt God's presence, guidance and strength. Decisions had been made, stands taken, and decisive turning points reached when our congregations sought to be faithful. We realized that each congregation existed in a local, national and global community, all of which were undergoing continuous change.

Brian Fraser's book helped us to engage in a process of knowing our story alongside the Biblical story. It helped us address the question "What does God want us to do or be?"

Different experiences of congregational life gave rise to different images and metaphors for the church. For example "we are like a high school band with several missing sections; a whole wheat chocolate chip cookie (nourishing and wholesome, but with some delicious bits); a stir fry (mixture and variety, but each part retaining its own colour, texture and identity). The traditional metaphors that spoke most strongly to people were those of the body of Christ and a haven in a heartless world.

The study helped us to identify the way we saw ourselves, but also called us out beyond ourselves. We are all ministers and need to be proactive in our ministry to the community and the world around us.

The final phase, "Proposing an Alternative Future," invited the whole congregation to a special retreat day. Using a planning process, we developed a number of proposals, based on our findings, to give our congregation new directions. We decided to act on three of the proposals.

First, we wanted to make the congregation more visible in the community. So we put up new signs, did some landscaping, hired an interior decorator to give us a new look, and included advertising in the church budget. It's worth noting that our goal was not to increase in size. We also changed the name *back* to Deer Lake United Church from Central Burnaby because it better defined our location in the community. We like being a relatively small congregation, in a small church; we just didn't want to shut ourselves off from the neighbourhood.

Second, we decided to begin a ministry for and with youth. Within six months we hired our first youth minister.

And third, we wanted to pay more attention to the gifts that people already had. Initially, we tried to compose a computer database of people's gifts. After a year, we abandoned this rather static process,

and started working on a more flexible and dynamic model for enabling people first to identify, and then to offer and develop their gifts.
Thus we started with the gifts that people had, rather than the gifts we
thought we needed.

The Vitalization Program did two important things for Deer Lake
United. It did not automatically launch us into either a building or a
fund-raising project or an evangelism campaign. And, rather than make
us feel guilty about what we are *not*, both as a church and as individuals within the church, it helped us to affirm what we *are*.

*David Martyn was Minister of Deer Lake United Church for ten
years before being called to First United Church in Kelowna,
British Columbia. During his ministry in Burnaby he played an
active role in the neighbourhood including publishing a newsletter
for the Burnaby Hospice Society, chairing the Parent Advisory
Committee of a local school, and helping to launch a Multifaith
Council.*

Some new church developments result from analysis of community needs and demographics. Others, like Westdale United in Peterborough, Ontario, result from one person's vision that there simply ought to be a church here.

15

Volunteers make the difference

by Georgina McKenzie

When a new church starts up, many folk find themselves doing unexpected tasks of service and administration. At Westdale United, one of those people was J. Edgar Peters. Mr. Peters, a retired financial administrator, faithfully conveyed the information for each Sunday bulletin to a neighbourhood typist who produced the church bulletins on an ancient Gestetner. With never-failing cheerfulness, he would present the hymn numbers and scripture readings to her with the pronouncement: "This is the drill for next Sunday!"

Edgar Peters was hosting a meeting of the trustee committee in his home when he was seized by a fatal heart attack. During the warm autumn day in 1983, Mr. Peters had been busy preparing information for the evening meeting. He was renowned for meticulous preparations for any meeting; he was always ready with the appropriate "drill" for every occasion, yet he was impatient with unnecessary "fuss and bother."

He may have sensed his imminent death. In a conversation prior to the meeting, fellow trustee Girv Devitt commented upon the tidy arrangement of chairs in the spacious living room of Mr. Peters' condominium, high above one of Peterborough's main thoroughfares. Mr. Peters' replied, "Yes, I'm happy to have this large area around me — I shall be occupying a much smaller space soon."

Dr. Jim King remembers the tragic event well. "It was for me a hail and farewell experience," he says. He had been urged by Mr. Peters to become a trustee. That night, Dr. King was attending his first — and last — meeting with his host. Dr. King, with Girv Devitt, performed pulmonary resuscitation upon Mr. Peters, reviving him several times. However, he did not survive.

An act of intuition

Mr. Peters' involvement in the formation of Westdale was an interesting twist of fate. Years before, in Winnipeg, he and his family had been well known to the man who was the prime mover in Westdale's formation, the Rev. Dr. Barry Day, minister at Trinity United Church in Peterborough.

Is a church the result of a visionary's dream, a community's need, or a viable proposition? Any or all of these could apply to New Church Development.

In the case of Westdale United Church, in the west end of Peterborough, Ontario, a church was certainly one man's dream. Dr. Day, the energetic and visionary minister of Trinity in Peterborough, dreamed of a church in this developing area. The established churches in nearby neighbourhoods, however, would have disputed that it was a community need. But a new church was thought to be a viable proposition because of planned real estate development in this part of the growing city.

Peterborough, with a population of 67,000, is an interesting mix of industry and tourism. It is home to plants of General Electric Canada and the Quaker Oats Company, and gateway to the famous Kawartha Lakes tourist region, which is next door to the equally famous Haliburton Highlands. It is a city of beautiful parks, and a lake centred by an illuminated fountain. It has both the Otonabee River and a portion of the Trent Canal System within its boundary. Peterborough is also home of Trent University — grey limestone buildings on a campus that spans both banks of the river and embraces an ice-age drumlin.

Westdale did not result from demographic surveys or statistical projections, though. Dr. Day was simply convinced there was a need for a United Church in the area. So, for a three month experimental period in the spring of 1982, he, Josephine Mewett (an elder at Trinity), and Diana McLeod, Trinity's organist and choir leader, conducted services in a public school in the Westdale area. Six couples who lived in the area but attended churches in other parts of the city also assisted.

The experimental stage made Dr. Day more and more confident about a new congregation. While serving Trinity United Church for 14 years, Dr. Day had watched the city expanding westward. Intuitively, he felt the promising possibilities of a church in the west end.

Not everyone shared his optimism. There was honest fear in the hearts of many that a new church would be formed from membership lost to other established churches. Presbytery shared this concern.

Often expensive surveys are the basis for decisions for New Church Development. Dr. Day favoured a direct approach — hold worship services and see what happens. This forthright action was typical of Dr. Day. Recognized as an able administrator, Dr. Day admits to a desire to "be in the driver's seat," but, he ruefully remembers, it isn't always so. His enthusiasm has, he confesses, occasionally led him astray. He tells of the time he and his wife, Lilia, were moving from one home to another. Dr. Day made innumerable trips back and forth between the two locations with his car and a rented trailer. During one really hurried trip, he thought he should check on his load, so he hopped out, gave a few tugs on the ropes and, satisfied that all was as it should be, leaped back in and couldn't start the car. It was only after a few frantic moments of confusion that he realized he was sitting in the back seat!

Steps along the way

By the summer of 1982, there was sufficient interest to warrant reclassifying the experiment as a "mission project." With the approval of the Peterborough Presbytery and under the supervision of the Rev. Cameron Reid of St. Matthews-Donwood Pastoral Charge, planning meetings were held over July and August in the home of one of the supporting couples. During these meetings, a church name was chosen, the services of a retired minister were obtained, and the rental of the school auditorium (for worship) and one classroom (for nursery) was extended by the Peterborough Board of Education for the following year.

Thus Westdale United Church was launched.

The first shepherd of this small flock, the Rev. Frank Whiteley, was a kindly gentleman whose smile, twinkling eyes and great sense of humour endeared him to young and old alike. His hobby of carpentry and love of fine wood grains has been a practical outlet for his boundless energy.

Promotion of the new church ranged from flyers delivered to neighbourhood households by members, to newspaper articles and radio and TV advertisements; from posters in area stores and businesses, to delivery of information to targeted areas by Canada Post for a small fee. There was even an article in *The Circuit Rider* (the Bay of Quinte Conference insert in *The United Church Observer*).

All the usual organizations of a United Church were established: Sunday school, choir, women's groups (one of which, as it was mainly composed of young working women, enjoyed the unusual name of "Ladies of the Night"), and the official board (session and stewards). Members of the first official board were Brian K. Earle (chairperson), Ross Graham (treasurer), Judy Graham (secretary), John Bardsley (recording steward) and the chairpersons of the Church Trustees, Elders and Stewards.

Many of the "furnishings" of the new church were gifts. John Bardsley made a cross. Edgar Peters, before his heart attack, donated a communion table that, when stripped of its dark finish years later, revealed a blond wood identical to that of the new pews of the sanctuary. Communion cups came from a city church that was about to discard them; bun baskets for the offering and a quantity of the old blue hymn books also came from another church's discards. All of these were faithfully stored in a cupboard under the stage in the school auditorium, after each service, by Gordon Millett.

Early funding for the church took many forms, such as garage sales, card parties, dances and dinners, and social activities among the members. Gifts of money, offering boxes made by Bill Copeland to replace the baskets, a pulpit from Keene United Church, choir gowns from St. James' United, more hymn books, communion plates (a memorial gift from the Bardsley family) and brass candles, cross, and altar vases from the Peters' family were accepted with gratitude.

Fund-raising events were also fun-raising occasions with laughter and high spirits. In later years, after the church was erected, Girv Devitt, a much respected lawyer in the city, sacrificed his beard for pledges. A food tent at the local exhibition became a major yearly fundraiser. Because it is fully wheelchair accessible, the church is used by many groups in the community. An active catering group has gained a notable reputation by providing excellent meals and refreshing coffee breaks for many outside organizations who rent the church premises.

To finance the actual building, the church received a block grant from the Bay of Quinte Conference and a Ventures in Mission loan from The United Church of Canada. The financing plan for the church anticipated significant support from the local Presbytery to supplement the VIM Loan. When Presbytery was unable to provide this support, the congregation obtained a bank loan in order to complete the church building.

The new congregation builds its own traditions

Traditions, such as an annual church picnic, began while the congregation still met in the school auditorium. Christmas pageants also started early, and involved much ingenuity from Sunday school teachers and parents and great performances by the Sunday school children. Any occasion was an opportunity for fellowship, fun, good food and laughter. This *joie de vivre* carried over into later times with kite flying at the church site, a hot air balloon at the sod-turning ceremony, and Victoria Day fireworks celebrations called "Holy Smoke."

Music was always an important part of both worship and fun. Under the leadership of Margaret Fleming, a small but dedicated choir sang at each church service. At any and all celebrations there were parodies of songs with words composed specifically for Westdale people and events by Marg and her husband, Bob.

For the Flemings, this was their second new church venture. They had been involved in New Church Development in Pointe Claire, Quebec. Marg was originally from Peterborough; she married her engineer sweetheart, and then lived happily for 26 years in Pointe Claire. When Bob's employment brought him back to Peterborough, Marg was very reluctant to leave her happy lifestyle and music in Pointe Claire. Bob therefore commuted for 16 weeks, driving home for weekends in Pointe Claire and living during the week with the Rev. Frank and Helen Whiteley. After Frank agreed to be minister of the new church, Marg was enticed back with an exciting proposition — another brand-new church experience as choir leader, this time with Frank as minister, and Helen and Bob as "the choir"!

The congregation was formally constituted by the Peterborough Presbytery on February 27, 1983, with 101 members. A draft Statement of Purpose for the congregation — this was long before the current fad of "Mission Statements" — included the following tenets:

- To provide a place of worship ... and to promote the spiritual growth and well-being of the congregation and of the community;
- To provide opportunities for sharing the Gospel of Jesus Christ ... by supporting the Mission and Service Fund of the United Church;
- Through a program of Christian Education, to assist in the world outreach of the United Church;
- To provide opportunities for community service through youth groups — Guides, Brownies, Scouts and Cubs, as well as the United Church's own Explorers and CGIT ... — and through women's, men's and senior citizens' groups;
- To seek out the social needs of the community;
- To become, more and more, a living expression of the Christian commitment, concern and faith.

Finally, building begins

In February of 1984, after a survey of all households in the area, 6.4 acres were purchased — a site on one of the highest points of land in the area. The negotiations for this purchase, which took nine months, involved many meetings with Peterborough Presbytery and with the Corporation of the City of Peterborough because of needed extensions of services such as sewers, water and electricity. Future plans for this acreage included, as well as the church building, the sale of four lots and the provision of seniors' housing.

By this time, a change in venue of church services was required. The congregation "graduated" from the public school to a nearby high school, where recess bells did not sound during the sermon and the prayers, and sports equipment did not hover overhead or protrude from the walls!

In September, Frank Whiteley, who had nurtured the new congregation from its inception, retired (again). The respect and love that the congregation had for their minister, as well as the camaraderie shared, were displayed at a gathering in his honour. On that occasion, a poem dedicated to Reverend Whiteley commemorated his "quirk" of forgetting the choir's anthem; it was called, "Perhaps This Would Be A Good Place For The Anthem!"

The Rev. Dan Yourkevich was then called to Westdale. He found, upon his arrival, that a Sunday school of 50 children flourished and mid-week activities such as the meetings of the Session, Stewards, and Trustees, as were the gatherings of women's groups and Hi-C (the high school and university youth group). "Rev. Dan," a young father of three children, quickly found his place in this new congregation. Fresh from other church building projects, he set himself to the task of increasing the community's interest in the new church. In his own words, Rev. Dan's personal commitment to stewardship education made him "the right person in the right place at the right time" for this phase of Westdale's journey.

Rev. Dan remains certain that "emphasis on the support of the Mission and Service Fund of The United Church of Canada, while facing extraordinary financial needs locally for a new building, was and remains a key to doing ministry that is not self-centred." Before Westdale was building a physical building, its support of the Mission and Service Fund surpassed that of churches that had been operating long before Westdale.

Once again, the fund/fun-raising events produced wondrous results. One year after the mortgage for the land was assumed, the debt was discharged and the mortgage burned at a jubilant morning service.

Early in 1986, the growth within the congregation was projected to rise from 220 to 340 in the next four years. Much optimism was felt. The economy was robust. The promotion skills of the full-time minister were evident in Rev. Dan's tireless door-knocking in the surrounding community of 3200 homes.

The "construction" year (1987) brought forth another side of the congregation. Not only did these people know how to have fun and raise money but they possessed many building skills. Basic planning for the construction of the new church had occupied the waking and sleeping hours of the building committee and its chairman, Bob Fleming, for more than a year. The group was somewhat surprised that The United Church of Canada had neither suggested building designs for new churches nor recommendations to offer. The plan for the new church, selected after countless expeditions viewing new church buildings and talking to members of other new church congregations, was based on Glencairn United Church in Kanata, Ontario. The services of Brown, Beck and Ross Architects were contracted. The completely wheelchair accessible building, constructed at ground level throughout, now includes, besides the sanctuary, a large many-windowed gymnasium/hall next to a fully equipped kitchen, Sunday school rooms, nursery, washrooms, offices and choir room. There is also an overflow room isolated from the sanctuary by sliding glass doors and equipped with remote speakers. Parents of "voluble" young children often choose to be seated in this room when their youngsters, for some reason, do not wish to play in the bright, supervised nursery with its Sesame Street decor and toys.

Raising time, talent, and treasure

A visitation program, complete with illustrations of the building plans, requested pledges of volunteer labour, special skills, and financial commitment. All members — business leaders, homemakers, engineers, teachers, minister, retirees, and teenagers — seized shovels, moved building materials, mixed cement, climbed ladders, hammered nails, painted, cleaned, laid carpets. As one member said, "You name it, we did it!" An average of 30 people worked on weekends, with retirees George Duffin and Bill Copeland applying their special woodworking skills during the week. Many were the snacks consumed — the soup and sandwiches, the coffee, the butter tarts. Anxious eyes watched the weather and the calendar...

Generous support for the new building was given by members, individuals and other churches in the gifts (many in memoriam) of chancel furnishings (communion table and chairs, pulpit, lectern, pulpit Bible, baptismal font and paraments), piano, and oak cross, to mention only a few, all chosen in accordance with the interior design. Even grocery store tapes were saved diligently for tableware! In later years a stained glass window was commissioned and installed by Dawn Straka as a memorial to her husband and members of her family.

At long last came the day of the dedication of the new building. The celebration culminated, in the afternoon, with a "better-late-than-never" laying of the cornerstone.

Minimal staff means dependence on volunteers

After Rev. Dan accepted a call to another congregation, Westdale had about a year of various interim ministers, before the Rev. Joan Henderson accepted the call and began her ministry to Westdale in 1989. "Rev. Joan" came to Westdale from nearby Keene United Church, bringing with her youthful enthusiasm, a loving yet practical viewpoint, and a strong Christian philosophy.

Westdale's church staff has always been minimal: minister, secretary and choir leader/organist. Upon Marg Fleming's retirement, the tradition of inspirational music was continued by Gwen Woodcock, hired in March of 1992. Lynda Henson was the first church secretary followed in April of 1990 by Connie McCracken.

To supplement their ministry, Westdale United Church has been blessed by many loyal, capable volunteers. Some have been in the public eye, such as board chairpersons Brian Earle, Terry Dunford, Mae Smith, Robert Wigle and Dawn Straka. Others, not as visible, include neighbourhood friend, Jan Schoenmaker, who cares for the building and grounds; Gord Millet who mows lawns in summer; Bob Neesom who clears the snow in winter; and Marion Edmunds who faithfully "puts the coffee on" each Sunday for the after-service fellowship time. Days and days of landscaping labour created lawns. Trees and shrubs, donated and planted by church members, are cared for on an annual Arbor Day. Indoor plants thrive in the sanctuary, narthex and kitchen, nurtured by Joan Dooher. Housecleaning days are scheduled for spring and fall and day-to-day cleaning is provided by members as funds are not available to hire a janitor. New furnishings, such as extra Sunday school cupboards and classroom clocks, are made by the skilful hands of Cliff Palmateer and Ron Dooher.

The strong fellowship among charter members is now shared by new members and continued use of skills and the resulting visible accomplishments provide immense satisfaction.

Into an uncertain future

The financial picture today is not as bright as one would wish. The downswing of the economy and resulting job losses, and the lack of anticipated development in the area adjacent to the church have brought financial difficulties. The problem has been accentuated by the inability to sell four lots, as originally intended, to reduce the overall debt load. However, off-setting these concerns is the fact that the bank loan has been eliminated, the VIM loan has been reduced significantly, there are more contributing members and envelope givings have increased.

This portion of the Westdale story spans the period of Easter 1982 to June 1996. At this point in its 14 year history, Westdale has a strong commitment of its members to the care and maintenance of its building and property. The Beaver, Cub, Scout, Sparks, Brownie, and Guide affiliations continue to thrive. There is an admirable "presence" (the food tent) at the local annual exhibition and a growing outreach into the community (in the schools and at a seniors' residence). Annual over-subscribed Mission and Service givings, an active Sunday school and youth group, Confirmation classes, baptisms, a dependable lay-ministry element, Presbytery representation — all indicate a continuing fulfilment of the original congregational purpose. In addition, the Bethel Series of Bible study was completed by two groups, and an active prayer chain, of six women and one man, prays daily for those who request this service.

Dr. Day's initial dream has been realized. The beautiful church structure and the strong fellowship of believers testify to that. There are still many hard workers. True, some of the pioneers are gone and many others are tired. However, there appears to be a nucleus of youthful adults who are willing to carry the dream onward.

To this end, a "dream committee" proposed by Bob Wigle, former chair of the Official Board, has reviewed the original dream, the present situation, and the promises of the future. In particular, there will be a special focus on possible uses of the balance of the church property. Options still to be considered include one of the earlier concepts of seniors' housing.

The strength, caring and faith-founded resourcefulness of this young congregation was sorely tested by the sudden death of its beloved young minister. A few days after a retreat with women of the congregation at Camp Quin Mo Lac (the United Church Camp on Moira Lake), Rev. Joan underwent minor surgery. After a week of extreme pain, death by pulmonary embolism came to this valiant, young Christian woman. This tragedy, in December 1995, shocked the Peterborough community and caused the Westdale congregation to search deeply for the resiliency to carry forward the plans and vision of their young friend, counsellor and sister in Christ.

Encouraged and aided by Rev. Joan's husband, Warren Morrison, several members of the congregation sought healing in a series of grief sessions led by full-time supply minister, the Rev. Louise Graves. Once again "the right person in the right place at the right time" can be the description of Graves' ministry to Westdale. The needed guidance and inspiration has been provided for a deeply hurting group. A pastoral relations committee began, in 1996, the task of calling a minister. In the meantime, under the enheartening and forthright leadership of "Rev. Louise," Westdale reaches into the future.

Canada's society is no longer as church-oriented as it was. The future of The United Church of Canada and of newly established churches, such as Westdale, will probably be quite different from the "dreams" of the founders of our national church in the year 1925. Time will tell — but what has been accomplished thus far must surely count in God's scheme of things.

Georgina McKenzie is a transplanted Western senior, originally from Chilliwack, B.C., who has God-given passions for people, pets and prose.

Pilgrim United in Victoria had a church, but no congregation. The challenge has not been to build a building, but to build a people. To do that required going back to some basic theological principles.

16

Pressing on without maps

by KEITH HOWARD

A story from the first century BCE may be apocryphal, or it may be true:

Back when much of the world was unexplored and unknown, not surprisingly, global map-making was a rudimentary and inexact science. When map makers drew their maps, they represented the area outside of their knowledge with symbols of dragons, monsters, and large fish. The message was clear; the uncharted and unknown territory was a fearsome place. It was a region touched with terror, a realm to be avoided.

One commander of a battalion of Roman soldiers was more adventurous than fearful. Eventually, he found himself beyond the territory that the map makers had drawn. Being a well-trained military man, he neither wanted to turn back nor to recklessly pursue his course without further instruction. Immediately he dispatched a messenger back to Rome with the urgent request, "Please send new orders, we have marched off the map."[1]

At Pilgrim United, we are not off God's map, but we are in unknown territory. The break we received in 1988 — when all but two people left the congregation over the controversy then splitting The United Church of Canada — has provided us with an immense new opportunity.

Unlike many situations of new development, Pilgrim United was left with a building but few people. Our task was not how to acquire a new building but how to build a Christian people.

Our current members are not burdened with any historic understandings of how things ought to be done in church. Most of them come with no previous church connections. Therefore the dragons of denial do not devour our energy. Current small numbers mean we are more like a sleek sailboat, supple and quick, ready to respond to the breeze created by God moving among us. But so many winds blow, which should we catch? More fundamentally, which course should we set?

Fundamental convictions

Conventional wisdom has it that these are tough times for the church.

Predictions of doom point to falling numbers of both members and worship participants, decreasing financial resources, a loss of confidence in church leaders, and a corrosion of denominational prestige among the general population. These realities pointed to the first, and most basic of the decisions facing Pilgrim Church — whether or not to continue. In consultation with presbytery and conference, the decision was made that the situation post-1988 warranted grief, anger, mourning and confession — but not despair.

Four fundamental convictions shape this response and our subsequent ministry:
- The world belongs to God. Death and despair do not rule;
- God is present and active in the world seeking to bring about shalom for all of creation;
- God is always opening up new possibilities;
- We are called to be partners with God in the working out of God's salvation. We have a mission.

Discerning congregational mission

"The church exists by mission, just as fire exists by burning." states Emil Brunner.[2]

As a New Church Development (or redevelopment) congregation, Pilgrim United Church openly courts guests. Because of the pressures of finance and the desire of members to feel they are doing the
right thing supporting this fledgling group, strong temptation exists
to view guests as potential notches on the Membership Roll. Or, as
Dick Moffat and Harry Oussoren write, "to greet newcomers and have
them sense that they are being welcomed more for their mortgage-
servicing capability than for their part in the community of worship,
learning, witness, and outreach."[3] The gravitational drag of finances
proves immense. Effective resistance needs to be rooted in a clear vision of our true purpose. Growth cannot occur without clarity of purpose.

Theologically, misconstrued mission constitutes heresy. And, to
borrow a psychological phrase, heresy leads to dysfunctional ministry
or just plain unfaithful living. False mission leads ultimately to despair.

Our starting point for mission — which we declare rather than
argue — is God. God is on the loose, seeking to bring to completion
that which was begun at creation and revealed in Jesus the Christ.
"Neither the world nor the church sets the agenda or the demands for
Christian ministry, lay and clergy. On the contrary, God calls us to
leadership and the gospel must shape our response."[4]

The order is clear: God, world, church.

The call is communal. This affirmation has consequences. The
temptation of any New Church Development is to slant the gospel
and the mission of the church so that it can be marketed effectively. In
its most crass form, it proclaims: "Have we got a deal for you! Feeling
lonely, discouraged, unfulfilled? Come, join us, and you will find fulfilment and joy in service." The claim may be true, but the order is
important. The church and congregations do not exist to offer low
cost, alternative paths for self-fulfilment.

The fundamental affirmation of the church as participant in God's
mission to the world may cause discomfort. Or, in more devastating
terms for a young congregation, it may offend some people who might
otherwise be willing to bring their bodies, children, and money to the
organization.

Dancing to the beat set by God also means that the church cannot
become too wedded to particular forms of past ministry. If God is indeed on the loose, initiating and responding to change in the creation,
then flexibility and surprise become part of the church's life. At Pil-

grim, therefore, we try to be as conscious of "getting out of the way" of God's spirit as of creating programs.

Lyle Schaller urges congregations like ours that seek to "reach and serve the generations born since 1942" to "build their ministry around the concepts and values reflected in such words as grace, relationships, hope, love, forgiveness, identity, acceptance, compassion, choices, caring, and service."[5]

The historical and biblical records of the Christian church provide a multitude of mission themes.

Our proposal for a statement of congregational mission is that we, as people of Greater Victoria, are called together by God under the oversight of The United Church of Canada, to co-operate in God's work by:

- nurturing in people a vibrant, life-changing faith in God as known through the person Jesus,
- encouraging individuals to be involved in God's work in the world and providing a corporate means of co-operation, and
- foreshadowing the kind of community that God envisages for all of God's creation.

Tracing the three strands of purpose

Though, in many ways, the three strands of this mission statement weave together, the first emerges as a strategic concern.

Old Testament scholar Walter Brueggemann talks of the need to restore memory to those inside the church. "The crisis for 'the insiders' in our churches is that abundance and affluence have caused church members to be distanced in self-sufficiency from the power and cruciality of the memory, so that the church suffers from profound amnesia..."[6]

We seek to respond to "outsiders" who are entertaining the possibility of becoming "insiders." While this moves evangelism and hospitality up the ladder of our concerns, it does not remove the necessity of creating an environment and structures that communicate clearly not only the kerygma but also the traditions of our theological, biblical, and ecclesiastical heritage.

The second strand of our statement affirms that God calls us, as a community, into a new world, to give allegiance to God and God's new way of being.

Church growth, while not an unfaithful goal, must always be subservient to and congruent with God's work in the community.

The third strand — of foreshadowing God's community — seeks to highlight the necessity of reflecting in our own life and practice the principles of respect, fairness, justice, and compassion to which we are, at times, so eager to hold others accountable. In more biblical language, it seeks to hold us accountable so that our relationships are righteous.

Within the framework of this statement of mission, several goals emerge:

- to develop as a congregation, and participate in, as worshipers, meaningful worship experiences;
- to promote opportunities where we as a congregation and individual members may be of service to others;
- to engender a warm, hospitable congregational climate where both members and guests feel warmly welcomed into the community of the people of God;
- to nurture a climate that encourages people to think about their faith and how the Christian gospel relates to their life;
- to encourage a sense of community where people are both supported and held accountable by fellow pilgrims.[7]

Evangelism

As a young congregation, we are acutely aware that, numerically, our hope for organizational survival lies in our ability to share the good news of Jesus Christ. We are also very aware of our desire — and the denomination's desire for us — to attract sufficient people to make us viable. Theologically, these pressures mean that issues of evangelism and hospitality are near the top of the heap.

Evangelism is not hospitality, nor can it be equated with church growth, though all are related. Fundamentally, evangelism is not a program but an attitude. Christian evangelism — coming from the Greek work meaning "to announce the good news" — declares, though word and deed, a message of hope and change that transforms life from the level of amino acids to the furthest galactic nebula.

Clearly the biblical announcement is more than "Come to our nice, friendly, neighbourhood church where we are open to all kinds of people, lifestyles, and faiths." The specifics of the message fall to the preacher and the congregation to work out, but the radical implications can not be denied, no matter how strong the temptation "to invite people in, with the winking assurance that 'everything' can remain the same."[8]

The least that our small band of Christians at Pilgrim United Church want to say is that the good news of Jesus Christ to which we witness offers possibility and the hope of new life.

In the language and images drawn from the current fascination with narrative, we have a Bible full of transformational stories and a congregation full of people who knew next to nothing about the Christian church being transformed by the story of God in Jesus Christ. "Evangelism means inviting people into these stories as the definitional story of our life, and thereby authorizing people to give up, abandon, and renounce other stories that have shaped their lives in false or distorting ways."[9]

Evangelism is risky because we dare to say that the socially accepted paths to the good life lead to anything but life. Our announcement constitutes an act of defiance.

In recent decades, we in the British Columbia Conference of the United Church have shied away from the boldness of this proclamation, fearing we might sound imperialist or triumphalist or exclusive. But evangelism does not have to be either triumphalist in tone, or militaristic in style, or brusque in manner. We can, as in New Testament times, simply witness with enthusiasm and conviction to how we have been transformed in Jesus Christ, and what we have experienced.

In the final analysis, evangelism should follow the rhythm set by the One who first came with Good News. He came with an invitation, not with coercion. The smell of snake oil does not have to surround our witness. We simply declare, through word and deed, the way of Jesus, and we testify that "this account of lived reality is more adequate than rival accounts that are given to us in the alternatives of secularism and legalism that are all around us."[10]

Such bold evangelism drives us back to foundations. For such proclamation has a cracked cornerstone if it is based only on the variety of congregational programs, the attractiveness of our leadership, the beat of our music, or the beauty of our building. If, when all is said and done, both the congregation and the members do not have a sense of life-giving and life-changing holiness in their innermost being, no amount of program or papers, of refinancing or restructuring, will lead to new life.

There are many ways and means of evangelism. From a preacher's point of view, struggling with appropriate formulations of the gospel is crucial; from a teacher's point of view, working to help others think about and integrate their life with the Christian faith is paramount. Today, as always, witness flows as much from walking the Way as talking about the Way.

Hospitality

Usually the encounter follows worship. The inquirer, alone or with support of family, asks about joining the church: "We really like it here. What do you have to do to join?"

The question has many levels. On one, it seems to be about integration and membership. And it is. But it is also about faith development and hospitality. For the question, however gently put, pushes issues of the theological boundaries of the congregation.

Much of what makes Pilgrim United a good congregation is its hospitality — the warm atmosphere, the feeling of acceptance, the many implicit messages that a person counts, that they are missed when they are not there. We want to be a warm, welcoming congregation. But how does the desire to be hospitable mesh with the need for boundaries? The discussion has begun.

Some — usually refugees from other denominations or victims of past exclusion by a more rigid church — say that "openness" must mark our congregation. Hand in hand with "being open" seems to go a reluctance to establish any boundaries at all. Though no one explicitly declares it, a moral imperative seems to hover that "We must not establish any boundaries that might lead people to feel that they are unwelcome." We are not, of course, universally consistent about this principle. We do not, for example, hesitate to set moral boundaries about such actions as wife-beating, sexual abuse, violence, or other dehumanizing behaviour.

Others argue that part of the real content of Christian faith is the mandate to be hospitable and welcoming. At issue then is the content and limitations of hospitality as a theme for ministry.

Hospitality does not preclude standing for something. The key question, in any community, is not whether there will be boundaries, but how will those outside the boundaries be treated?

Brueggemann says that, in the early period of biblical history, the outsiders — often named Canaanites — were, as a general rule, "those who are committed to (or trapped by) socio-economic practices at variance with covenantal ethics, who practice religious symbolization that supports such practices."[11] One perpetual response to outsiders, says Brueggemann, was vengeance — forced conformity or destruc-

tion. The basic attitude prevails even among those advocates of social
justice who leave others only two options: "agree totally, confess and
repent; or turn away in anger or sorrow."[12]

Hospitality is the biblical alternative to vengeance. Biblical hospitality far outstrips the current etiquette of being "nice" or "gracious."
Implicit in the biblical view lies the moral imperative to engage the
outsider, the ones excluded, excommunicated, and banished.

Brueggemann names the three movements of God's dramatic saving acts in and through the strangers:

- The gift of power for life given outside the control of the empire depends
  on the stranger bringing hurt, hate, and grief to public speech in the
  midst of a community;
- God expresses solidarity with outsiders;
- Through the intervention of Yahweh, the God who hears the cries of the
  stranger, the outsider acquires a new status. The outsider, in solidarity
  with Yahweh, is called to a new life in freedom that the empire cannot
  give or deny, an obedience that the empire cannot compel or prohibit.
  The new status as an insider is commonly referred to, in the Old Testament, as being "chosen."[13]

Given such memory and expectation, hospitality thus becomes one of
the defining marks of God's people.

Hospitality is an orientation born out of memory of the Christ and
of the initial encounters of God's people with Yahweh. "You shall not
oppress a stranger; you know the heart of a stranger, for you were
strangers in the land of Egypt" (Exodus 23:9). The rhythm of the God
who chooses sets the pace for a hospitable church. If we are to be a
hospitable congregation in the biblical sense, our ministry must dare
to bring to speech the hurt and grief of our community; to call upon
the God who alone can save; and to dare to claim for ourselves and
the "outsiders" the status of beloved of God.

The first task is not maintenance of the church as institution or
recruitment to increase the number of identifiable givers. The task is
"to tell the non-person, the non-human, that God is love, and that this
love makes us all brothers and sisters."[14]

Hospitality thus emerges as one key test of the church's faithfulness to God.

Hospitality also grows out of hope. One of the lessons of the past
is that God is often encountered in and through the stranger. "In every
encounter with every stranger," says Parker J. Palmer, "we are given

the chance to meet the living Christ."[15] Hospitality "offers a rich opportunity for meeting someone new, being challenged by different perspectives, and possibly being transformed. Just as the stranger may need us, so we may need the stranger."[16]

A place of hospitality creates a safe and welcoming space for persons to find their own place, their own sense of humanity and worth. As Henri Nouwen says, "Hospitality is not a subtle invitation to adopt the lifestyle of the host, but the gift of a chance to... find their own."[17]

Those who are attempting to push the church toward new images and metaphors of mission find a crowd of candidates for "outsiders" to whom the church is called to be bridge-builders or hospitable, in the biblical sense:

- Every 14.5 minutes, someone reports a new AIDS case.
- The world has 1.6 billion persons with handicapping conditions, 80% of whom live in the Third World. One-third of these are children. If all the deaf and the blind in the world lived in one country, it would be the seventh most populated country in the world.[18]
- The collegiality of building bridges to strangers is a metaphor for missional ministry that opens endless opportunities for caring evangelism and service. Whether it is Alzheimer's or AIDS, whether First World or Third World, whether male or female, whether lay or clergy, whether liberal or conservative, whether rural or urban, whether straight or gay, whether white or Native American, whether bishop or bartender, no non-persons populate the inclusive family of God. God's eye is on the sparrow.[19]

Hospitality is not just a way of providing emotional and social service types of support. Spiritually it means intentional cultivation of the virtues of compassion and generosity. It means opposing rising climates of fear, for frightened people are rarely peacemakers. A hospitable church stands against the deadly disease of xenophobia — "the fear of strangers, foreigners, and outsiders."[20] In a time of decreasing economic and social expectations and continuing racism, this proves no small challenge.

Serious engagement of a ministry marked by hospitality will mean more than making sure greeters are on hand Sunday morning to say, "Hello, nice to have you with us." In our community, it may well mean taking the risk of continuing to rent space, at a reduced rate, to a Teen Centre, where outsiders with baggy pants, long hair, and too-loud music can find a safe place. It may mean becoming more proactive about seeking out other groups within our community — battered women, AIDS victims, physically and mentally disadvantaged people, Aboriginal people, young adults — and finding ways to convey the message that they are loved by God and by us. The implications are many, and will have to be worked out by the community. Even the existing architecture of Pilgrim United may need modification if hospitality really becomes a priority.

"In 1990 the corridors in church buildings need to be much wider to encourage informal conversations and fellowship, to be utilized as channels of communication, to make strangers feel welcome, to facilitate people-watching, to help convey a distinctive congregational image, and also to serve as pedestrian walkways."[21]

Hospitality thus emerges as a fruitful metaphor for part of our ministry. Hospitality reminds us of the value of those not in the centre of the circle of societally-deemed respectability and worth. We are always called beyond ourselves.

Joining the church

Both evangelism and hospitality are outward-facing in that their prime concern is not the addition of new bodies in the pews. Their primary motivation is thus distinct from church growth. However, in the exercise of our witness and ministry of evangelism and hospitality, it may be that there will be some who would like to become part of the community. Questions of integration then arise.

Why should people want to join a congregation? There are many reasons — good influence for their children, they feel lonely, they like music, etc. Theologically, though, the question pushes at the purpose of the congregation.

Pilgrim United's purpose may be seen as having three facets. People, trying to respond to whatever presence of God they sense in their lives, seek us:

• to nurture their faith. Often people might not name the various urgings, longings or other feelings of dissatisfaction that lead them to our congregation, but it is not too much of a stretch to think that God may be in those feelings and that people, in trying to respond to those feelings, seek to know and grow in faith.

• to engage together in activities that express and deepen their faith; activities that are not available to them as isolated individuals. Many people are sensitive to concerns surrounding God's creation, youth, poverty, or those grieving the loss of a partner or a significant relationship.

They come, in part, to find like-concerned people who can, together, discover ways to respond to the needs of creation and community.
- to experience a community of hospitality where relationships are marked by respect, justice, and compassion. Sometimes people come from abusive situations, they come suffering from psychological, spiritual, and physical wounds, and they seek a safe place where they can be recreated and remember their name as beloved of God.

Predictable patterns

At Pilgrim United Church, we have observed at least five different components of a person's walk with the congregation:
- the initial visit to the congregation,
- subsequent visits, often at varying intervals,
- semi-regular attendance at worship combined with some involvement in congregational activities or programs, perhaps even the assumption of a job or function within the congregation,
- an articulated desire for activities that deepen faith, e.g., Bible study, Christian education programs, retreats, etc.,
- formal affiliation through membership.

The three latter components are not necessarily linear. Most simply seek involvement; they see little benefit or need to become a member officially. Others "join" through transfer of membership or affirmation of faith before they indicate any desire to grow in the faith. Each component has its own set of challenges and opportunities and, obviously, one component cannot and should not be confused with the other. People who come back for a number of Sundays may or may not want to be integrated with the congregation.

Observation of this process does not settle the theological questions about membership or integration. The reality is that most who come to our congregation are biblically, theologically, and ecclesiastically illiterate. We may make follow-up phone calls and sends cards when we notice guests at worship, but what do we hope for these guests — other than solicit their regular attendance at worship and their financial commitment? Framed as a question of discipleship rather than a question of filling pews, in what areas should they grow in skills and knowledge if they are to become more faithful disciples, and not just part of the club?

Our fledgling Session developed some signposts that we use to help people find their way on the path to a more intentional and faithful discipleship.

We recognize the journey of faith as a life-long process that each person walks at their own pace and in their own manner. Yet we seek to point to some things that Christians have found key to discipleship. We offer these areas of interest not as rigid criteria that must be checked off in the manner of passing an examination, but in the spirit of guided discovery. The tone we wish to strike is that we take discipleship and membership in the church very seriously. We seek not to erect walls but to provide springboards for discovery and growth.

Session has roughly divided these concerns into four areas: worship, the Bible, church mission and history, and personal faith development. We are working towards an apprenticeship model where people explore each of these areas with an elder, who then assists them in reflecting on various dimensions of that activity.

Worship
- Knowledge of the general outline of a worship service and the function of each component of a traditional worship service,
- Knowledge of how the sacraments of baptism and Holy Communion are celebrated at Pilgrim United Church,
- Knowledge of the purpose and history of the sacraments of baptism and Holy Communion,
- Introduction to worship planning.

Bible
- Knowledge of the overall Biblical story,
- Knowledge of the purpose and location of key types of literature contained in the Bible,
- Knowledge of the general historical background of the various parts of the Bible,
- Knowledge of at least two different ways in which the Bible may function in moral decision making,
- Introduction to how the Bible may be used as a worship resource,
- Introduction to how the Bible may be used as a resource for personal spiritual development.

Church Mission and History
- Knowledge of the history of The United Church of Canada,
- Knowledge of the symbols contained in the crest of The United Church of Canada,
- Knowledge of the political structure of The United Church of Canada,

- Knowledge of the political structure of Pilgrim United Church,
- Knowledge of (and, we hope, some participation in) mission activities beyond the local congregation,
- Knowledge of the mission statement and goals of Pilgrim United Church.

Personal Faith Development
- Knowledge of the various "spiritual gifts" given to the church,
- Discovery of and reflection upon one's own gifts and talents,
- Knowledge of stewardship as a model of the Christian life,
- Discovery of and reflection upon personal struggle,
- Discovery of and reflection upon areas of personal growth,
- Discovery of and reflection upon personal beliefs and commitments,
- Discovery of and reflection upon unresolved questions and concerns,
- Encouragement to participate in an ongoing (daily) spiritual discipline.

A sense of belonging

While this sets the framework for expectations and development as a disciple at Pilgrim United Church, there is no guarantee that work on these areas will issue in a sense of belonging. According to Schaller, "There is considerable evidence to suggest that at least one-third, and perhaps as many as one-half, of all Protestant church members do not feel a sense of belonging to the congregation of which they are members."[22]

What, then, specifically fosters a sense of belonging to this community, given our cultural context?

The Search Institute of Minneapolis recently completed a study of 11,122 people in 561 randomly chosen congregations within the six major mainline denominations in the United States — Christian Church (Disciples of Christ), Evangelical Lutheran Church in American, Presbyterian Church (USA), Southern Baptism Convention, United Church of Christ, and United Methodist Church. The results of their study have proved helpful as we have struggled with identifying the marks of a faithful and hospitable congregation concerned to nurture faith. The following are the marks we have identified to date:

We seek to share in God's work by developing quality, uplifting services of worship.

Through worship we hope, in the language of narrative, that we will see our story in the light of the story of God in Christ. In that light, we will then be able to live with hope, forgiveness, and joy. As

people are able to see their story in the light of both God's story and
the congregation's story, a sense of oneness grows.

**We seek to share in God's work by developing and maintaining an
effective Christian education program for all ages.**

The Search Institute names this as the central component of congregations that effectively nurture faith.[23] We are committed to such a
program, but, to date, have run into many obstacles placed in our
path by an alien culture: competing demands for time, lack of training
in the Christian faith for most of our congregation, and a lack of confidence for people other than clergy to lead any kind of Christian education event. Our hope is that as people grow in knowledge and skill
in the areas noted above, they will feel more confident as disciples and
as part of God's people.

**We seek to share in God's work by fostering a thinking climate in
which people are encouraged to reflect on their faith and relate
their faith to their lives.**

Such a climate is not restricted to formal Christian Education
events, but must be present at all levels and all areas of congregational
life. People must be free to identify, voice, and struggle with fundamental and persistent concerns if they are ever to feel equal partners
in the congregation.

**We seek to share in God's work by providing opportunities for peo-
ple to engage in service to the wider community.**

Not all express their faith the same way. For many in our congregation, it is critically important to provide concrete, hands-on, per-
son-to-person service opportunities. In this area, at least, our experience seems to harmonize with Schaller's observation that "the congregations that have the best record on the assimilation of new adult members offer a variety of meaningful contemporary goals in which the
new members can relate, support, and become involved in very easily
and very quickly."[24]

**We seek to share in God's work by developing structures and poli-
cies that reflect respect, fairness, flexibility, accessibility, and compassion.**

The secular language uses terms such as a fair and just workplace,
but we aim for more as the people of God. We will fall short, but the
norm remains both as a goal and as a command.

We seek to share in God's work by fostering a warm, accepting environment where all feel welcome and valued.

The reflections above on hospitality find expression here, at least in part. We would like to be a community where "outsiders" can find a safe place filled with grace. That's the theory. It too, like all utopian visions, has the power to seduce us. However, the cultivation of such an atmosphere requires intentionality and caretaking, even for those already on the "inside." Seeking those "outside" will require even more commitment and courage.

We seek to share in God's work by developing a sense of family where people are known and cared about and have the opportunity and responsibility to care for each other.

Even 7-11 convenience stores train their people to greet each individual who walks through the door — and all they ultimately want is for the consumer to return to purchase again. We strive for the development of people who have the character and skills to care for one another. Like all other marks, this becomes a community responsibility, though some may take particular responsibility.

Not a pick-and-choose smorgasbord

These marks are dynamic. They exist in interdependence. There is no linear sequence, nor do we feel this is a smorgasbord from which we can pick and choose. Strategically, some items may require more attention than others at particular times, yet we seek to have them known by all.

While we can agree with Bill Easum, the American church consultant, that effective congregations of the future "look for ways to bond people to the values and goals of the congregation,"[25] we seek more than just ways to super-glue the people into the institution. People need to feel they are loved and valued, that they are growing in relationship and that opportunities exist for them to serve one another, God, and God's creation. We seek to be a community that nurtures the many and interacting relationships between God, people, and the creation.

The centrality of relationships has contributed to the popularity of cell-based or small group structures within new congregations. Bill Easum heralds such models as the wave of the future. However, almost all of the research is American, and seems captivated by the American mega-church model. While we may learn from this, it is not clear what is transportable to our particular Canadian context, and whether or not different understandings of authority and accountability might forestall wholesale adoption of some strategies.

One thing we do applaud in such models is the emphasis placed upon the Pauline concept of spiritual gifts. Ministry is a function of the entire community. However, a variety of gifts have been given to enable the whole community to minister and to allow individuals to live lives of joy in service.

One of our prime tasks in the next couple of years will be to develop instruments that encourage people to discover their gifts and that assist them to find opportunities to use and develop those gifts within both the congregation and the community. We want to find as many ways as possible for people to live as stewards of their gifts and to affirm the diversity of gifts and areas of service that God gives.

The affirmation of gifts is nothing new. Yet by affirming it as a basic emphasis of ministry, we hope it will shape the style of our congregation. We hope to "encourage people to develop their ministry around one or two of their strongest gifts instead of fitting into a particular ministry that the church requires."[26] Loren Mead correctly notes that one temptation of this approach is to lose depth and grounding, rather than to coerce and manipulate.[27] A ministry of gifts can deteriorate into each doing their own thing; we hope it will not. We aim for a community where each has a part, and each has responsibility in the mission given to the congregation.

Pilgrims always thrown back to the basics

Pilgrim United Church, in may ways, stands as one small tangible expression of both the opportunities and the challenges that face our church.

A large part of the challenge that faces us is that almost everything seems open for review   and all parts are interconnected. Not only do "external issues" like reproductive technology, communications technology, and a multi-cultural, multi-religious world pose huge theological issues but, at the same time, we deal with a rapidly shifting culture. Throw into the mix a review of organizational and management issues, and, at times, it seems one can hardly turn around — or attend a meeting — without some foundational issue being touched.

Pilgrim United Church has been rightly named. We are pilgrims, walking a new path while trying to be guided by traditional landmarks. We do not have all the answers. We may detour, stumble, and trip, but we are walking the Way of faithfulness as best we can. We live in hope.

*The Reverend Keith Howard currently serves as part of the minis-
terial team at Pilgrim United Church and as B.C. Conference
Minister (staff position) with responsibilities for Communications
and Global and Societal Concerns.*

1   Donald C. Posterski and Irwin Barker, *Where's a Good Church?* (Winfield, B.C.: Wood Lake Books, 1993), p. 213.

2   Quoted in Donald E. Messer, *A Conspiracy of Goodness: Contemporary Images of Christian Mission* (Nashville: Abingdon, 1992), p. 18.

3   Dick Moffat and Harry Oussoren, "Front Page," *The United Church Observer*, March, 1994, p.1.

4   Messer, *A Conspiracy of Goodness*, p. 44.

5   Lyle E. Schaller, *21 Bridges to the 21st Century: The Future of Pastoral Ministry* (Nashville: Abingdon, 1994), p. 34.

6   Walter Brueggemann, *Biblical Perspectives on Evangelism: Living in a Three Storied Universe* (Nashville: Abingdon, 1993), p. 72.

7   We have been greatly assisted in formulating those goals by the results of The Effective Christian Education Study. See especially Eugene C. Roehlkepartain, *The Teaching Church: Moving Christian Education to Center Stage* (Nashville: Abingdon, 1993), chapter 4.

8   Brueggemann, *Biblical Perspectives on Evangelism*, p. 130.

9   Ibid, p. 10.

10   Ibid.

11   Ibid, p. 49.

12   Terry Anderson, "No Defense Against Nonsense," in *Touchstone*, Vol. 11, No. 1 (January 1993), p. 18.

13   Walter Brueggemann, *Interpretation and Obedience: From Faithful Reading to Faithful Living* (Minneapolis: Fortress, 1991), p 297 ff.

14   Gustavo Guttierrez, *The Power of the Poor in History: Selected Writings*, trans. Robert R. Barr (Maryknoll: Orbis Books, 1983), quoted in Letty M. Russell, *Church in the Round: Feminist Interpretation of the Church* (Louisville: Westminster/John Knox, 1993), p. 26.

15   Quoted in Messer, *A Conspiracy of Goodness*, p. 104.

16   Ibid, p. 105.

17   Henri Nouwen, *Reaching Out*, quoted in Russell, *Church in the Round*, p. 173.

18   Messer, *A Conspiracy of Goodness*, p. 99.

19   Ibid, p. 108.

20   Ibid.

21   Schaller, *21 Bridges to the 21st Century*, p. 33.

22   Lyle E. Schaller, *Assimilating New Members* (Nashville: Abingdon, 1978), p. 16.

23   The implications of this study are outlined in Roehlkepartain, *The Teaching Church*.

24   Schaller, *Assimilating New Members*, p. 80.

25   William Easum, *Dancing with Dinosaurs: Ministry in a Hostile & Hurting World* (Nashville: Abingdon, 1993), p. 61.

26   Ibid, p. 74.

27   See Loren Mead, *The Once and Future Church: Reinventing the Congregation for a New Mission Frontier* (The Alban Institute, 1991), p. 47.

Glossary
of United Church of Canada (UCC) terms

"1988" — The 1988 General Council met in Victoria, British Columbia and passed a resolution that stated that homosexual persons were not to be excluded from ordination on the basis of sexual orientation. This issue revealed a variety of opinion throughout the church and some people and a few congregations even broke away from the UCC.

Bethel Bible Study — a two-year course developed by the Adult Christian Education Foundation in Madison, Wisconsin, a comprehensive overview of the Bible, comprised of four semesters of seven weeks each over two years of study.

Board of Home Missions — The former name of The Division of Mission in Canada (DMC). DMC is one of the five Divisions within the General Council office system (the church "head office" or "church house") and is responsible for national leadership in such areas as Family Education and Justice; Congregation, Mission Support and Rural Life; Human Rights & Economic Justice; and Worship.

Call — The formal invitation a congregation extends asking a minister to become their pastor. This process is done in consultation by the congregation with Presbytery.

CGIT — Canadian Girls in Training. An education and social organization for girls between the ages of 12 and 17, sponsored in part by the UCC. Badges are earned for various skills and studies.

Christian Education (CE) — Christian Education refers to both the Sunday school and Adult Christian Education programs of a church. Each congregation will usually have a committee of people to organize and administer the church's CE program.

Church Board or **Church Council** — The governing body of a Congregation or Pastoral Charge used where the Session and Stewards (Official Board) have merged. Also known as a Unified Board. The Board or Council is a more streamlined version of the Official Board. Instead of separate Session, Stewards and Official Board meetings, one meeting of all members is held. The Board membership includes the chairs of the church committees as well as the committee members. The Council membership consists of the committee chairs or representatives only. Congregations elect the members of a Unified Board and committees are formed from this membership. In the Council structure, congregations elect the committee chairs who form the membership of the Council. Committee members are then chosen by a variety of methods.

Church Redevelopment — A congregation undertaking a new direction in ministry rather than a continuation or expansion of existing work or a project that has the potential to initiate a responsive action both within the existing congregation and with others in the surrounding area. Such redevelopment is the result of a congregation-wide revisioning process.

Committees — the common UCC committees in each Pastoral Charge include Christian Education (CE); Outreach or Mission and Service; Finance and Property; Stewardship; Worship; and Ministry and Personnel.

Conference — a regional level of administration within the UCC responsible, among other things, for the care and support of Presbyteries. There are 13 Conferences within the UCC. All ministers within the Conference along with lay persons selected by Presbyteries meet annually or bi-annually to conduct the business of the Conference and make plans for the forthcoming year.

Ecumenical Decade — The decade 1988 to 1998 was declared "The Ecumenical Decade of Churches in Solidarity with Women in Church and Society" by the World Council of Churches (WCC). Member churches of the WCC can use the theme as a focus for their mission.

Elder — **A member of the Church nominated and elected by the congregation** to exercise spiritual leadership within the congregation and the community. Elders serve as a group that may be called a Session or may be the title of those who serve on Church Councils or Church Boards.

Explorers — A group for girls under the age of 12, with a similar purpose to the CGIT.

Extension boards or councils — Capital holding companies established by Conferences or Presbyteries to assist in the financing of New Church Developments.

General Council — The highest legislative body of the UCC, which meets every two or three years. Representatives from across the country, both lay members and ordered ministers, meet to discuss UCC policy, vote on new initiatives, and appoint an executive and sub-executive to be responsible for the work of the church between General Council meetings.

Hi-C — A UCC high school and university youth service and fellowship group, developed from the former Young People's Union.

Kairos — A biennial national conference sponsored by The United Church of Canada for young adults aged 18-30. The conference is designed for participants to grow in relationship with God, neighbour and self in an atmosphere of fun and friendship, warmth and worship, learning and laughter, and dialogue and dancing.

Kerygma — **An international (United States, Ca**nada, Australia and New Zealand), interdenominational Bible study program, centred in Pittsburgh, Pennsylvania. The name *Kerygma* is a Greek work meaning "proclamation" or "word proclaimed."

The Manual — The official book containing the laws and bylaws of the UCC. The book is revised and updated after each meeting of the General Council to reflect any changes to Church law made during the meeting.

Mission and Service Fund — Also known as the M&S Fund. This is the channel through which local congregations and the UCW contribute money to the wider church. The fund supports the work of the General Council offices, which includes programmes, overseas personnel, grants, development and relief projects, new church development opportunities, and a wide variety of local community services.

Mizpah Benediction — "The Lord watch between me and thee while we are absent from one another." (Genesis 31:49)

New Church Development (NCD) — A new community of faith in an area where there is a significant increase in population or a congregation overtaken by development e.g. an existing congregation in a village that has changed from rural to urban.

Official Board — The governing body of the Congregation or Pastoral Charge made up of the Elders (Session) and Stewards. The most local level of UCC administration.

Pastoral Charge — The local level of administration of the UCC. A Pastoral Charge may include one congregation or more (known as a "two-point" or "three-point" pastoral charge).

Presbytery — a localized unit of administration within the UCC, between the congregation and Conference, which usually includes approximately 20-50 pastoral charges. There are 94 Presbyteries within the UCC. A Presbytery is comprised of all ministers appointed to Pastoral Charges within its bounds, all ministers associated with special United Church ministries, retired ministers, and lay delegates appointed by congregations. Presbyteries meet anywhere from monthly to a few times a year.

Session — Those people within a congregation responsible for the spiritual life of the Church's membership and their ministry in the community. Found only in an Official Board model of church government.

Stewards — The management of a Pastoral Charge's financial affairs is the responsibility of the Committee of Stewards in the Official Board structure. With a Church Board or Council the Pastoral Charge's finances are managed through a Finance Committee. The Pastoral Charge also has a Stewardship Committee (or sub-committee) that is responsible for teaching the theology of stewardship and encouraging the practice of giving.

Tentmaker from Naramata — Naramata is a UCC Educational and Conference centre located in British Columbia. The Tentmakers program ran from 1981-1995 to train lay people for volunteer youth ministry (youth group leaders, Sunday school teachers, and so on). The name "tentmaker" was taken from the life of St. Paul, who was a tentmaker by trade and did not earn his living through his church work. The Tentmakers program was replaced by the Youth Ministry Certificate Program in 1996.

Unified Board — see **Church Board** or **Church Council**

United Church Women (UCW) — A service, study and fellowship organization for women within the UCC. Members of the UCW are organized into groups within local congregations calls "Units." United Church men also have their own group called "As One That Serves" (AOTS).

Ventures In Mission (VIM) — (see the Introduction for a full explanation) — A fund of the UCC for New Church Development capital projects, redevelopment capital projects for established congregations, and human resources and program needs for new or established congregations.

Watkins Fund — The Reginald Watkins Fund was established from his estate to further work on behalf of elderly people.

Congregational Resources
from The United Church Publishing House

A Faith to Live By
A Resource for Adult Study
by Frederick A. Styles

Fred Styles investigates the challenge of faith for life in the 20th century. This volume explores Creeds, God, Jesus Christ, the Holy Spirit, sin and salvation, the church, the Bible, baptism, communion, life after death, and humanity. Program notes by Marion Pardy round out this helpful study aid.
0-919000-66-5 $12.95

God Hates Religion
How the Gospels Condemn False Religious Practice
by Christopher Levan

Is the church a colossal mistake? Has institutionalized religion corrupted the original intent of Christ's mission? Must the church "die" in order to make room for new life? With a powerful, prophetic voice, Levan declares that God has cause for concern, even disappointment, with the covenanted community. Many of us sense that our faith could be much more; that it is crippled by bureaucracy and tradition. Levan asserts that the church can break destructive patterns and be renewed — but only if it is willing to risk its own survival for the sake of an egalitarian community, patterned after the gospel's vision of God's coming reign on earth.
1-55134-045-3 $15.95

Faithstyles in Congregations
Living Together in a Christian Community
by Wilena G. Brown

This volume provides an analysis of three faithstyles — community, searching, and partnership — found within all our congregations. Understanding the needs of each style can bring fruitful harmony and an appreciation of the gifts that each offers. A valuable aid for church leaders, outreach committee members, and all who engage in congregational life.
1-55134-006-2 $12.95

The Dancing Steward
Exploring Christian Stewardship Lifestyles
by Christopher Levan

Chris Levan, president of St. Stephen's Theological College, explores why we have trouble relinquishing our personal resources and introduces us to the three steps of "letting go"; solidarity, relinquishment, and expectancy. Questions at the end of each chapter make this a versatile and creative teaching guide for those wanting to explore the nature of Christian stewardship lifestyles.
1-55134-004-6 $14.95

Walking the Way
Christian Ethics as a Guide
by Terence R. Anderson

Terry Anderson, a recognized ethicist, invites readers to think about using Christian ethics as a guide for living well in a perplexing world. This is an ideal introduction to reflecting on the Christian way for students, church leaders and the general public.
1-55134-003-8 $18.95

The Future of the Church
Where are we Headed?
by Douglas John Hall

A personal look at the church from the view of someone who is just about the same age as The United Church of Canada. Hall calls this work "a biographical testimony" and uses his personal experience for the larger purpose of illustrating a more expansive analysis of our ecclesiastical sojourn.
0-919000-57-6 $13.95

This is Your Church
A Guide to the Beliefs, Policies and Positions of The United Church of Canada
by Stephen Chambers

Church members will find this book, revised and updated for the third edition, an excellent resource to help them express their faith more clearly, through increased understanding and information about out United Church of Canada. This is a book that reflects a church that continues to live and struggle with the gospel.
1-55134-027-5 $11.95

A Guide to Sunday Worship
by Alan Barthel and David R. Newman
edited by Paul Scott Wilson

A step-by-step guide, now in its third printing, through the Sunday service exploring the history and meaning of each part. Helpful to sessions, worship committees, choirs, membership classes, parents and candidates preparing for baptism, families who worship together, and anyone who wants to understand worship better or to help lead in worship. An ideal resource for enriching one's praise of God.
0-919000-38-X $10.95

Voices and Visions
65 Years of The United Church of Canada
edited by Peter Gordon White

A lively and informative history of The United Church of Canada — with contributions from John Webster Grant, Steven Chambers, Diane Forrest, Bonnie Greene, and Sang Chul Lee — that celebrates in words and photographs our first 65 years. This beautiful, full-colour coffee-table book is a welcome addition to home and church libraries and the perfect gift for all special church occasions. Winner of the 1991 Angel Award.
0-919000-52-5 $19.95

Taking Control of Your Mission Agenda
by Bonnie Greene

This book helps you to clarify your committee's role on the mission of the congregation, plan and carry out projects and, above all, prevent "mission fatigue." Greene's straightforward and practical guide explains how to set directions, understand the theology of outreach, and nurture vision within the congregation. An invaluable resource for outreach and mission committees, including work sheets and resource lists.
0-919000-64-9 $9.95

Me, A Representative to Presbytery?
by Deborah Laing

This is a "must have" booklet for lay people who become Presbytery representatives for their congregation. The book provides clear accessible information, not only about Presbytery, but about the other courts of The United Church of Canada, their relationships to each other, and how they work to carry forward the mission of the church.
0-919000-79-7 $6.95

Order Form

Congregational Resources
from The United Church Publishing House

SHIP TO:

Name: _____

Address: _____

_____

Phone: _____

Fax: _____

Title	ISBN number	Price	Copies	Total
A Faith to Live By	0-919000-66-5	$12.95	_____	_____
God Hates Religion	1-55134-045-3	$15.95	_____	_____
Faithstyles in Congregations	1-55134-006-2	$12.95	_____	_____
The Dancing Steward	1-55134-004-6	$14.95	_____	_____
Walking the Way	1-55134-003-8	$18.95	_____	_____
The Future of the Church	0-919000-57-6	$13.95	_____	_____
This is Your Church	1-55134-027-5	$11.95	_____	_____
A Guide to Sunday Worship	0-919000-38-X	$10.95	_____	_____
Voices and Visions	0-919000-52-5	$19.95	_____	_____
Taking Control of Your Mission Agenda	0-919000-64-9	$ 9.95	_____	_____
Me, A Representative to Presbytery?	0-919000-79-7	$ 6.95	_____	_____

Subtotal _____

Shipping Charges $2.00 per book _____

In Canada please add 7% GST _____

Total _____

Payment is required with your order. U.S. orders must be paid in U.S. funds. Thank you.

Please mail your order with cheque to:
The United Church Publishing House
Dept. P, 4th floor   3250 Bloor St. W.
Etobicoke, Ontario, Canada, M8X 2Y4